DIABOLICAL

OR

PSYCHOLOGICAL

The Differentiation Of Psychological Diseases
From Diabolical Disorders

Segunda Yanez Acosta Ph.D.,
P.M.H.C.S., B.C.

To order additional copies of this book, contact:
Xlibris Corporation
1-888-795-4274
www.Xlibris.com
Orders@Xlibris.com
112555

CONTENTS

DEDICATION

This book is dedicated to God the Father, the Author of Life.

ACKNOWLEDGEMENT

I wish to express my deep appreciation to my daughter, Dr. Lealani Mae Acosta, who edited my work despite her hectic schedule in the hospital and for her professional insight into the clinical content of my writing. To my daughter, Mary for her proofreading, creative editing, and photography work.

To my loving husband, Leo, I wish to express gratitude for his hard work, support and devotion through all these years.

To my mother, brother and sisters, thank you for your love, fidelity, patience, and understanding.

To my spiritual director and devoted friend, Rev. Francis Peffley, Parochial Vicar, St. John the Apostle, Leesburg, Virginia and Spiritual Director, Arlington Regia Legion of Mary, who has patiently guided me and supported me in all my projects in the past 20 years.

My sincere appreciation goes to Rev. Franklyn McAfee, Pastor Emeritus, St. John the Beloved Parish, McLean, Virginia for his guidance, direction, and clinical discussions. He has truly been a mentor for me in the understanding of diabolical conditions and encouraged me in the writing of this book.

To my good and faithful friend, Rev. Bruce Nieli CSP, Paulist Evangelist and Missionary, who believes in me and inspired me to pursue higher ideals. He also assisted me in the editing of the book.

To my friend, Delores Nelson, my thanks for reviewing my manuscript and giving me constructive feedback.

To my assistant, Jill Rinke, thanks for her artistic editing of the drawing, and thanks to the other members of my staff for their encouragement and assistance in making this book possible.

To all my patients who have been my teachers in my clinical work, I thank them for their support of S.T.R.E.S.S. Centre Inc.

To all my beloved priests, religious, friends, benefactors, and relatives who have been there for me all these years, I thank them for their support and help in all my projects, especially, for the building of the Holy Trinity Jubilee Park Inc., as a center for evangelization and the only Catholic park in Northern Virginia.

FOREWORD

A young couple became very frightened and concerned, not only for themselves, but for their child and his grandmother living with them. The father and husband worked for a delivery service and had just leased a small house in a somewhat wooded section of northern Virginia. Ever since they had moved in, unexplained figures would appear on the bedroom walls at night. These strange figures were soon followed by eerie noises in the house, a source for which could not be found. The parents' fear turned to alarm as their five-year-old son spoke of his "friend" who came and played with him only at night.

In whom could they confide? Who would believe them? The climax of their terrible ordeal came at 2:00 in the morning with a crescendo of strange howls and loud, explosive sounds. Without hesitation, the father immediately gathered his family, loaded them into their SUV, and drove away. When they got near the end of the twisting road that was their driveway, the husband's work pager suddenly beeped. The eerie series of beeps punctuated the silence. He looked down at his pager and his breath caught in his throat as he realized that the call was coming from inside their house. The page read: "COME BACK." They did not go back. They never went back.

What this incident shows is that sometimes supernatural or paranormal activities cannot be explained by hallucinations, effects of drugs, sleeplessness, hypnopompic or hypnagogic activities, or an overly active imagination. I have dealt with people who would fall into any or all of these categories, as can happen in the case of concerned parents who see a demon under every bed or in every closet. One family even pleaded with me that their son was possessed because he would not do his homework or his chores.

But not every supernatural activity can be easily dismissed this way. There are a few, though not as few as people might think, bona fide demonic happenings as I believe was this case I shared in detail. We are dealing here with more than ghost activities: we are dealing with evil and personified evil. We are talking about demons and the devil.

Satan is not only a person, but a fallen angel with all the power that an angel has, with one difference—all this power is directed at you. He desires to torment, to annoy, and even to destroy you.

Exorcists have written books with scary narratives detailing multiple examples of demonic activities. Sometimes they also explain how this happens and how one can diagnose the activities. As far as I know, though, there have been no books and no manuals by a mental health clinician or a doctor that explain the phenomenon from a scientific perspective and how it should be treated.

Dr. Acosta's book is such a resource manual that any interested persons, mental health professionals, physicians, especially psychiatrists, nurses, the clergy and any persons involved in pastoral care, will find very helpful. Most importantly, it will be welcomed by those vexed by Satan and his demons, for it will empower people in the position to help with the knowledge of how to handle the situation and provide proper care, rather than backing away out of fear or ignorance. A comprehensive guide to discerning the psychological and the spiritual elements of psychiatric disease and possession has long been missing from religious and mental health literature—this book serves as just such a guide.

Reverend Franklyn M. McAfee, D.D., Pastor Emeritus, McLean, Virginia

DILEMMA IN FACING
BIZARRE CONDITIONS

"The face is the mirror of the mind, and eyes without speaking confess the secrets of the heart."

—St. Jerome

CHAPTER 1

DILEMMA IN FACING
BIZARRRE CONDITIONS

Contemporary culture, through such popular movies as the film *The Exorcist* (1973), *The Exorcism of Emily Rose* (2005), and the recently released film *The Rite* (2011), or one of the New York Times' best sellers, *Hostage to the Devil* (1992), is familiar with the phenomenon of diabolical possession of individuals. A key moment in these and similar media occurs when the possessed persons or their families realize that the symptoms exhibited by the possessed person cannot be alleviated or treated by medical or psychological treatment protocols, and subsequently turn to spiritual means for relief. This book is intended for mental health and medical professionals, as well as those involved in pastoral care, that are faced with such key moments, namely, when the practitioner begins to form the impression that the patient in front of him seeking medical or psychological assistance for mysterious, bizarre conditions is beyond that which medical science can explain and treat. This work does so by emphasizing the human person as a composite of body and soul, nature and spirit, a unity recognized by great minds, like Aristotle, Hippocrates, Plato, St. Thomas Aquinas, G.K Chesterton, or C.S. Lewis, to name a few. This natural view of the human person provides the client with reassuring and reasoned mode of self-inquiry and the practitioner with an alternate path in the examination of the seemingly inexplicable cases.

To be clear, the experience of the presence of evil in a client may never occur in most treatment settings. However when it does, such difficult to explain occurrences should rightfully set off warnings within the practitioner who must question this unexplainable discomfort. For example, personalities of a doctor and a patient may clash or personal ideologies may conflict. Yet the experience of the presence evil has nothing to do with a personal aversion for the character or lifestyle of the person seeking psychological care. The clinician experiences a forewarning that the patient needs help beyond what he can offer.

Some of the experiences that trigger feelings of being in the presence of evil can be any of the following scenarios. A patient switches personalities or appearances in a matter of seconds and there is neither known prior pathology nor any explainable psychological process attributable to the conduct. The client suddenly transforms into a seemingly different person, perhaps a person of voiceless cunning presence. Perhaps it could be a more startling transformation, such as the presence of a growling, contorted, blasphemous individual. In order to help highlight these and similar key moments practitioners may face when they experience such clients, this book details perplexing case studies experienced during my work both in an in-patient psychiatric hospital and within an out-patient private practice.

Although atypical and exceptional, the examination of the presence of evil can be approached in a clinical setting. When these cases are routinely rejected or dismissed by clinicians out of fear or lack of understanding of their patients, scientific inquiry is restricted, treatment approaches are limited, and client's choices are marginalized. This book attempts to familiarize clinicians, who may not consider other alternate causes for such bizarre behaviors, to the possibility that these types of patients can be helped by a methodical, valid and effective approach to treatment.

Back in 1972, I was working in a Catholic hospital's psychiatric unit when I recognized that some seriously mentally ill patients who appeared psychotic seemed also to suffer from something else that at that time I simply did not recognize. My clinical training certainly had no component that addressed major spiritual warfare. Nonetheless, there were observable symptomatic patterns in some patients indicating just such an internal struggle. These patterns included, for example, an inexplicable and powerful aversion towards religious objects, strength representing a force greater than what the patient was normally capable of producing or which was uncharacteristic for the patient. As a clinician, I wanted to explore all possible ways to relieve the patient's very obvious torment. One book, *Diabolical Possession and Exorcism*, expanded the inquiry.

> "Not long ago a psychiatrist friend of mine, for whom I have the greatest respect and whom I frequently confer with, told an interesting story. He had been discussing with one of his colleagues about the possibility of diabolical possession in certain cases. The other man found this unthinkable. A few weeks later, the latter was visiting a patient in a ward at the nearby state hospital. In this ward were a number of psychotic patients, potentially violent, who at that time were very subdued, some were asleep, others were walking around distractedly. The doctor was speaking with his patient, when a man neatly dressed in a business suit, white shirt, and a tie walked through the ward, "all hell broke loose!" The patients who were asleep woke up; those who were walking became belligerent and boisterous; and the help of the orderlies had to be solicited to restrain them. After calm had been restored, the psychiatrist asked the nurse, "Who was that man that walked through here before?" The reply was that it was a priest carrying the Blessed Sacrament to patients in the next ward. This caused him to have second thoughts about the possibility of diabolical possession." (J. Nicola, 1974, p. 47)

The above example, along with my personal experience, heightened my desire to understand the presence of evil in certain cases that were not simply treatable by conventional medications, psychotherapy, or even electroconvulsive treatment (ECT). Indeed, I questioned why was the psychological inquiry deliberately limited to that which can be explained by science? Can the clinician merely chart "of unknown etiology" and refuse to reach beyond psychiatry to address inexplicable presenting problems?

The questions I often asked myself and likely other clinical providers would ask themselves were: What are we dealing with here? Is there evidence of chemical imbalance? Is there a family history worth connecting? Are there illicit drugs involved? Did this person expose himself unknowingly to the occult? To answer these queries, a deep and thorough investigation is necessary. Every clinician confronted with these mysterious cases must be willing to explore other possible explanations. After twenty years of working with these types of cases, the reality is that the number of cases seems to be increasing rather than decreasing, and as such, the clinician needs to comprehend a basic understanding of diabolical conditions so that when faced by such a bizarre case there is a sense of familiarity on how to differentiate them and respond appropriately when help is not forthcoming.

THE ILLUSIONARY BATTLE BETWEEN
FAITH AND SCIENCE

"The truth and everything that is true represents a great good to which we must turn with love and joy. Science too is a way to truth; for God's gift of reason, which according to its nature is destined not for error, but for the truth of knowledge, is developed in it."

—Blessed Pope John Paul II

CHAPTER 2

THE ILLUSIONARY BATTLE BETWEEN FAITH AND SCIENCE

It was Saturday morning when I received a phone call from panic-stricken parents that their daughter who I had previously seen was acting bizarrely. The parents were afraid that the same thing was happening again in which previous hospitalizations did not help. They were begging to be seen immediately so that I could assess the situation and recommend proper action. I was seeing this young adult for depression after she experienced severe spiritual attacks, had been humiliated by those who prayed over her before, and was fearful of rejection from society that would label her as "weird." This demure, gentle, beautiful woman came into my office dressed provocatively, with clothes that were short and revealing, a face filled with overdone make up and lipstick marks on her cheek printing the numbers "666." She moved as if she were unstable on her feet, without control over her extremities, spoke like a drunk woman, was easily provoked to fight with everyone, and her voice was different from the normal voice I was accustomed to hearing when I saw her in therapy previously. I was shocked to see a totally different person, but prepared myself since I had been forewarned by the parents about what I was going to face. I knew she needed my help so I had to conquer my own fears. It was necessary to defend and protect this delicate patient from the attacks of the evil one. I instructed the parents to pray as I summoned some external help from my telephone tree of prayer warriors. I could not believe that every priest I tried to contact that morning was unavailable. My patient, shouting obscenities, rolled on the floor, while I grabbed my relic of the True Cross and my holy water, which I brought with me from home. I started praying, knowing I also was joined by others in prayer at that time. As I continued to pray, I noticed my own patient was trying to fight the evil by praying aloud with me. Finally she prayed completely the Healing and Protection Prayer composed by Rev. Bob Hiltz, T.O.R. (Exhibit A), which she had memorized from praying it so often. After three hours of intense prayer, the young woman got up from the floor with a smile and we praised God together, recognizing the triumph of our Lord Jesus Christ over demons. She went to the bathroom, washed herself and returned the same gentle attractive lady I had known. The parents were shocked and hugged their daughter. The father started asking questions about what happened. I, in turn, asked him what he had witnessed. He was cautious in responding since he could not explain what he had seen. He then asked me how I might explain scientifically what just transpired. I paused for a moment, then said, "For those who believe, no explanation is necessary. For those who do not believe, no explanation is sufficient." I started asking if any medication was given to his daughter. He said, "No." I then asked him what interventions had been done for her. He then replied, "Prayer." His perplexed face betrayed his disbelief at what he witnessed with his daughter, and how questions were running through his mind since he needed a tangible explanation to what he saw. It was necessary for me to explain to him how the brain works so I could give him ideas on how neurons work and the interplay of neurotransmitters play a role in emotions and behavior. Medications play an important role in the regulation of these neurotransmitters, which then help improve the patient's thinking and behavior. In other cases medications are beneficial, but not in this case. Prayer, with subsequent psychotherapy, plays a stronger role in the long term improvements of patients. Science could not directly explain what transpired that morning: only God was the answer. His wife and daughter, both practicing Catholics, were fully convinced that God came miraculously to help her from the grip of the evil one. He, on the other hand, was not a practicing Catholic, was involved in daily pornography, and needed some hard facts to explain to him what happened. He demanded a reasonable explanation in order to convince him. I had no other explanation. Nevertheless, in the end he was happy to see his daughter restored to her normal and interactive self.

This father is not alone. The rest of society is looking for a scientific explanation for miraculous events that take place all over the world. We are in such a high tech society that demands more data for the supernatural events. Despite the modern perception that religion and science are at odds, the Church encourages systematic and in-depth inquiry, including a rigorous investigation of apparent miracles. These two fields are not mutually exclusive. While appreciating the role of each, life in itself is a mystery that cannot fully be explained. No matter how hard man tries, God unfolds more mysteries each day.

How can we explain possession? The Bible teaches that man is made in the image and likeness of God. Man is comprised of body and soul. The body is the material substance that the human eye can see, while the soul, which is a spirit, is unperceivable to the human eye, but the very essence that keeps a person alive. Without the soul, we have a cadaver. With the soul, we have a living human being. Another Christian truth is that man is given free will to make a choice between good and evil. When evil completely takes over a human person, then we have a possession. A person may or may not be aware of the movements and speech coming out of himself, but in either event, something else outside of the self creates those things. The person can fight to regain control of self, which was what happened in the cited case. However, when evil has completely taken over, the fully possessed person has no recollection of the entire incident other than what witnesses convey to the person after recovery from the incident.

> "Evil is like a parasite which destroys its good host. If it could totally destroy its host, it would also destroy itself. Evil is inherently self-destructive. This metaphysical fact explains the otherwise puzzling empirical fact of humanity's amazing resiliency. Time after time, after falling into some deadly evil, we bounce back, the evil dissipates." (P. Kreeft, 1990, p. 217)

Where does science come into play with all these? The reality is that instruments can only do so much. This spiritual phenomenon is intangible and immeasurable. We can perceive with our senses and instruments may measure our responses. How do you measure a miracle? How do we measure grace? Scientific instruments try to measure and predict the intensity of a tornado, an earthquake, or a hurricane, but man cannot control these natural disasters, no matter how hard he tries. God remains to be mysterious and is the only constant explanation for all of these. We can not leave God out of the equation since He is the Master of the entire universe with more power than any created creatures, including demons, and more mighty than any man-made destructive force, such as the nuclear bomb.

> "It is no less evident that the peculiar basic truths of each inhering attribute are indemonstrable; for basic truths from which they might be deduced would be basic truths of all that is and the science to which they belonged would possess universal sovereignty." (Aristotle, 1952, p. 104)

GUIDE TO PROPER
DIAGNOSTIC WORK-UP

"Few souls understand what God would accomplish in them if they were to abandon themselves unreservedly to Him and if they were to allow His grace to mold them accordingly."

—St. Ignatius Loyola

CHAPTER 3

GUIDE TO PROPER
DIAGNOSTIC WORK-UP

A thorough diagnostic work-up includes a number of steps. These include an in-depth, face-to-face interview, psychological testing as applicable, ruling out of other possible causes, and final diagnostic formulation.

How does a clinician delineate a psychiatric case from a diabolical case? The first task of every clinician is to fully assess what is going on with a patient and nothing replaces an extensive, in-depth, face-to-face interview with the patient. A prudent clinician will pursue first a thorough investigation of the clinical presentation of the patient in order to formulate a tentative diagnosis.

I was recently asked to return the call of a patient who was struggling with demonic attacks and was in desperate need of help. She called from out of state and begged for immediate attention. I finally had a chance to call her back and this woman started unloading all the horrible experiences she had with allegedly demons attacking her. I listened to her story patiently, but I suggested for her to be seen in person so I could assess the true picture of her condition. While talking to her on the phone, she was so convincing about the events in her daily life that led to a number of priests praying over her. However, upon meeting her in person, I caught sight of a fast moving, fast talking, high energy, impatient, attention-seeking woman whose eyes revealed the same intensity of a bipolar patient. Red flags were raised. I proceeded to ask more questions. The husband revealed a roller-coaster life with highs and lows. His wife would only reveal to the outside world the high-performing parish volunteer, but she would disappear in her bedroom when depression sets in so no one had seen her this way other than the immediate family members. By the time I finished my interview with her and her husband, I confirmed my tentative diagnosis of bipolar I condition.

INTERVIEW

During the interview, not only can the clinician observe verbal and non-verbal cues, but pointed questions may be asked to give a better background of the history of the condition. The patient's spouse, parents, close relatives or friends are excellent sources of information to clarify the history further. The predisposing and precipitating events that led the person to seek help may be explored. A good family history also helps in looking for genetic, environmental, and spiritual connections that will assist in the formulation of a diagnosis. A thorough interview and initial work-up may include, but is not limited to, the following:

a. Presenting problems with signs and symptoms, frequency, intensity, factors that magnify or minimize the problems, other concurring problems, such as marriage issues, work issues, financial issues

b. Previous background including the onset of symptoms and types of treatments sought to relieve the problems

c. History of prescribed and non-prescribed medications, vitamins, supplements, eating/drinking habits, smoking, use of illicit drugs, what worked or did not work

d. History of other medical conditions or previous surgeries: when, where, and who performed them

e. Family history, presence or absence of psychiatric, medical, or substance abuse history, drawing of family tree, number of marriages, children, miscarriages, abortions, adoptions, deaths

f. History of trauma, physical, emotional, or sexual abuse

g. Description of self, relationships, friendships, work, relocations, meaningful people or aggravating people in the life of this patient

h. Appropriate psychological testing results, if available

i. Available medical records and other vital information from family members or significant others

j. Educational, work related, and social histories
k. Summary and evaluation with DSM IV-TR Coding for: Axis I, Axis II, Axis III, Axis IV, Axis V
l. Recommended treatment plan, signing of patient-clinician contract, and eventual discharge planning

What are the most frequently asked questions to help understand the problems of the client and can help define the clinical diagnosis of the patient? Every new patient undergoes a comprehensive assessment. The following are the most frequently asked questions of every patient:

- What is the presenting problem?
- What problems brought the patient to seek consultation?
- Who is identifying these to be a problem?
- What are the signs and symptoms being presented? How severe are they and how frequently are they occurring?
- How long have the problems been present?
- What was the earliest recollection of the client that there was a problem?
- Have these problems been present as early as childhood or adolescence? When did the first symptoms appear?
- What actually happened at the time the symptoms occurred? What was going on in the life of the person? Were there major changes or sources of stress?
- What kind of treatment was sought?
- Was there any medication prescribed? If so, how much and what was the effect?
- How long was the medication taken? If it was stopped, why was it discontinued? Who prescribed the medications?
- What are the current medications?
- Was there any counseling sought? Where, when, and who was the clinician?
- If counseling was discontinued, what was the reason? Who really made the decision?
- Was there any previous hospitalization? If so, when, where, what was the diagnosis and what treatments were rendered?
- What were the benefits and disadvantages of the hospitalization in the perception of the patient?

- Is the client taking any vitamins, herbs, or over-the-counter drugs? For what reason are they being taken and for how long? What are the effects on the client?
- Does the client have any allergies?
- Is the client a smoker? If so, what kind and for how long? If the tobacco use has been discontinued, how long ago?
- Does the client drink alcohol? What kind, how frequently, and how much? If the alcohol use has been discontinued, when was the last drink?
- Is there misuse or abuse of alcohol? Is there professional help or some type of support group?
- Are there any illicit drugs involved? What type and how frequent is the use? If stopped, how long ago? Did the person seek professional help or join a support group?
- Are there other illnesses present? Treatments sought or rendered?
- Are there significant past histories important for the clinician to know related to the problem, e.g., physical or sexual abuse?
- What are the previous surgeries? When and where?
- Describe childhood, adolescence, young adulthood, and adulthood.
- Describe relationships, education, relocation, and major events in the life of the person.
- What seems to alleviate the presenting problem, even if only temporarily?
- What seems to aggravate the presenting problem, even if only temporarily?
- How often does the problem occur? How long does it last?
- Are there any patterns or cycles involved in the condition?
- How is the condition affecting the person, the family, education, or work?
- Is there any significant family history connected with the presenting problem?
- Is there any psychiatric or substance abuse family history? If not diagnosed, were there relatives who were described by others as having unusual behaviors or personalities? Diagram a family tree.
- How does the person cope? What are the available support systems?
- Does the client profess any particular religion?
- Is the client an actively practicing this religion? If so, with what congregation is the client worshipping?

- Is the client a baptized Christian? If so, what is the religious denomination?
- Has the client been exposed to the occult?
- Has the client been involved with the New Age movement?
- Has the client been preoccupied with horror or violent movies, video or computer games, or books?
- What are the hobbies or interests of this client?
- How would the client describe himself? What pertinent personal information could be shared to benefit the clinician in understanding the case?
- Are there significant people in the life of this person who can shed light on the nature of the problem? Who among these individuals needs to be interviewed?
- Why is the client really seeking help?
- Even if the client does not think there really is a problem, can the client identify other areas that for which psychotherapy may be of benefit?
- If the problems were resolved, what outcome does the client hope to achieve? What will be the end result of therapy?

Patients should be asked to sign a medical release to allow the clinician to discuss matters with those who can provide valuable current or past information about the patient. A release form should include a waiver of the confidentiality of information, as well as Privacy Act Practices, and Patient Rights, which are discussed with the patient.

DIAGNOSTIC TESTING

Observation of the patient's behavior is continued in subsequent visits. Detailed notation of the speech patterns and content with signs and symptoms are made. Most patients undergo a variety of psychological tests, such as Beck's Depression, Hamilton Anxiety, Stress Audit, Symptoms Checklist, and other similar tests. Referral for more extensive testing could be done. The patient is given feedback on the results of all testing and observations with a tentative diagnosis. It is highly recommended that patients who demonstrate high level of symptomatology and have strong evidence of biochemical imbalance be referred to a psychiatrist for appropriate follow-up and medication prescription.

In many cases, the primary care physician is involved and informed as requested by the patient so that the clinician may work closely with the prescribing doctor for appropriate treatments and medications. The parents or the family may be involved depending on the age of the patient and to the degree and extent that the condition may affect the family.

RULING OUT OTHER CONDITIONS

There are certain rules I use in screening my patients, which are reviewed in the following stages:

- Rule out genetic transmission to see if biochemical imbalance is a likely possibility. This requires serious investigation of each side of the family, both maternal and paternal sides. For adopted persons, any knowledge of the biological parents is crucial in the formulation.
- Rule out chemical abuse or use that could impact the manifestations or magnify the symptoms of the client, including the use of over-the-counter medications, which also can be abused.
- Rule out other medical conditions that may interfere with or aggravate the present condition.
- Rule out environmental factors that could complicate the presentation, such as the presence of verbal, physical, and sexual abuses; any traumatic incidents in the past; any major familial events that may have affected the person such as separation, divorce, deaths, and adoption.
- Rule out unhealthy hobbies and habits that may affect the signs and symptoms, such as sleep patterns, eating habits, etc.
- Rule out the presence or absence of a support system, such as with whom the person lives, how close are immediate family members, who is the most significant support of this person, does the person socialize, is the person isolated or living alone, etc.
- Rule out psychological conditions that may interfere with the functioning of this person.
- Finally, rule out the possibility of a spiritual condition. Most clinicians may not have encountered a diabolical case before. For the benefit of those who may want to find out more information before conferring with a clergy, it is suggested to look into the possible exposure of this client to the occult, diabolical activities, fascination with games or

movies that unknowingly expose the person to open the door/s to the evil one. The findings in this section are best discussed with a clergy who can provide proper guidance to a clinician. (See Exhibit B)

DIAGNOSTIC CRITERIA

After a thorough interview, observations, review of past medical records, interview with significant family members, review of testing results, the clinician must complete the International Classification of Diagnosis (ICD) codes, that is, identify the specific diagnosis of the condition/s affecting the patient leading to the completion of the following:

Axis I   Primary and secondary diagnosis
Axis II   Developmental or personality disorders
Axis III   Physical or medical conditions
Axis IV   Source and level of stressors
Axis V   General adaptation level or level of functioning

The next major revision of the *Diagnostic and Statistical Manual of Mental Disorders* (DSM-V) will not appear until 2013. However, for those interested in looking at the possible changes in diagnostic categories, www.dsm5.org is a valuable site to follow-up query and updates on any work done thus far. DSM-IV was published in 1994 which led to a revision of DSM-IV, called DSM-IV-TR, published in July 2000. The primary goal of DSM-IV-TR was to maintain the currency of the DSM-IV text, which reflected the empirical literature up to 1992. Thus, most of the major changes in DSM-IV-TR were confined to the descriptive text. Changes were made to a handful of criteria sets in order to correct errors identified in DSM-IV. (American Psychiatric Association, 2000). In addition, some of the diagnostic codes were changed to reflect updates to the International Classification of Diseases, Ninth Edition, Clinical Modification (ICD-9-CM) coding system adopted by the U.S. government.

Although not as well received as his first book, *The Road Less Traveled*, Scott Peck's book *People of the Lie*, explained that it is crucial that conditions are labeled so that once the disorders are identified; there is knowledge on how to treat it. It is not merely for the sake of labeling, but also for the purpose of proper diagnosis and consequent therapy. This in turn provides a place for the diagnostician to ponder and explore the well documented diagnoses as well as to think outside the box. A serious observation of the presenting problems, quiet prayerful reflection on the stated symptoms, and self-evident signs presented at the session with a critical look using one's "clinical eye" will help pin down the actual problem of the patient. For the benefit of those who need to review the clinical symptoms of psychiatric illnesses, Appendix C contains the signs and symptoms of the most common conditions often confused with diabolical conditions. The list was not meant to include all psychiatric diseases, but the more typical conditions that can easily resemble diabolical conditions.

As noted earlier, nothing replaces a thorough diagnostic work-up that leads to a definitive diagnosis. In order to receive proper treatment, a diagnosis must be made appropriately, and it needs to be based on facts and grounded in reality. The tension lies in the patient's perception, which contradicts or denies reality. This is the root of the psychiatric patient's disease. The truth is illustrated albeit humorously by G.K. Chesterton who made the following observation about a madman's grasp of reality:

> "The madman is not the man who defies the world; he is the man who denies it . . . . All delusions have in them this unalterable assertion—that what is not is. The difference between us and the maniac is not about how things look or how things ought to look, but about what they self-evidently are. The lunatic does not say that he ought to be King; Perkin Warbeck might say that. He says he is King. The lunatic does not say he is wise as Shakespeare; Bernard Shaw might say that. The lunatic says he is Shakespeare. The lunatic does not say he is divine in the same sense as Christ; Mr. R.J. Campbell would say that. The lunatic says he is Christ." (G.K. Chesterton, 1987, pp. 316-317)

Although this example is a bit tongue-in-cheek, we need to remember such humor in our work if we are to survive dealing with such complicated, demanding cases every day. However, our work is indeed a serious matter. If, after a comprehensive analysis of all the history, interview, observations, diagnostic tests, and other relevant information, but the client still does not fit the typical profile of the varied diagnostic categories, then a responsible clinician needs to pursue what is unavoidable. A respected professional must gather other types of data that could be a plausible explanation for the patient's weird presentation before conferring with clergy who can assist with the problem.

It is imperative for every clinician to be thorough in the psychiatric evaluation and diagnostic work-up since the report created by the clinician will be the basis for the subsequent action of the clergy and the appropriate referral to the Bishop whose decision will be affected by the content of the report. Every author who writes about diabolical conditions refers to appropriate evaluation by a mental health professional, even more specifically and preferably by a psychiatrist before any conclusion is made that a condition is definitively diabolical, not psychological. My experience in many cases is that there is co-morbidity. This means that the patient may suffer from a psychiatric condition and a diabolical condition at the same time. Many cases are not simply clear-cut psychological conditions only or diabolical conditions only. This is where an experienced clinician must clarify the observed signs and symptoms and distinguish one from the other.

SCREENING FOR SPIRITUAL WARFARE

"The devil strains every nerve to secure the souls which belong to Christ. We should not grudge our toil in wresting them from Satan and giving them back to God."

—St. Sebastian

CHAPTER 4

SCREENING FOR SPIRITUAL WARFARE

The majority of patients referred to me have various forms of psychological problems. The problems could be emanating anywhere from personal stress, marital stress, work-related stress, or other types of issues. If the patient has suffered from a condition for a long period of time before seeking help, his problem has caused maladaptive behavior requiring intervention. Most of these patients respond to the typical medical and psychological interventions. Some doctors also refer patients to me with debilitating physical conditions, such as diabetes mellitus, hypertension, headaches or other types of pain, since typical medical regimen did not cause improvement and there are underlying psychological problems that need to be addressed to clear the impediments to healing. There are others who have some type of unexplainable spiritual conditions that a relative or a priest recognizes as needing further evaluation. These cases have not responded to any psychotropic medications and standard psychotherapy despite repeated attempts. Discernment is crucial in differentiating spiritual warfare from a psychological condition. The clinician is faced with the reality of needing to assess what is going on with the client whose signs and symptoms defy the typical psychiatric illnesses.

"It is important for clinicians to be sensitive and knowledgeable regarding spiritual and philosophical beliefs. Professionals need to be capable of distinguishing normal, healthy spiritual growth from psychopathology . . . Such a distinction might depend on the

ergotropic/trophotropic balance created by the experience or by the alterations in the functioning of the brain structures subserving the holistic or causal operators. However, the fact that the spiritual exercises have an effect on the autonomic function as well as other cortical mediated cognitive and emotional processes suggests that such experiences not only affect the human psyche, but also may be utilized to assist in the therapy of various disorders. "(A. Newberg, 1998, p. 91)

In assessing a person, I try to determine what is going on currently with the patient and what went on in the past that may still be affecting the patient. As a mental health clinician, I am put in a position to provide feedback to a referring priest to determine if indeed the psychological or some other plausible explanation can be ruled out leaving only the spiritual condition as the explanation for the bizarre behavior. For any clinician who may not have encountered a diabolical case before, may I suggest that the professional seeks consultation with a member of the clergy. If the clergy is not comfortable dealing with diabolical cases, seeking help from a Catholic priest in their jurisdiction may be beneficial because there are individuals trained within the diocese to deal with such matters. It may also be beneficial to speak with a clinician who has dealt already with spiritual cases. I recommend screening for any familial or personal exposure to the occult or the New Age Movement in order to understand how the individual may have been affected. The tool that I have provided may be used in the assessment process, but if the clinician is not comfortable going in this direction, the practitioner may simply refer the client to a member of the clergy for further evaluation.

"Beloved, do not trust every spirit, but put the spirits to a test to see if they belong to God, because many false prophets have appeared in the world. This is how you can recognize God's spirit: every spirit that acknowledges Jesus Christ come in the flesh belongs to God, while every spirit that fails to acknowledge Him does not belong to God." (1 John 4:1-2).

According to Rev. Jordan Aumann, O.P. (1987), there are two types of discernment of the spirit:

"**Infused Discernment** is a charismatic gift granted by God to certain individuals. This a rare gift but when it occurs it is infallible because it is the result of an interior movement or inspiration received from the Holy Spirit, who can not err."

"**Acquired discernment** is a cultivated form of discernment complimentary to ordinary spiritual direction and can be cultivated by using the proper means."

He also added that "God inclines us to do good, working either directly or through secondary causes; the devil always inclines us to do evil, working by his own power or through allurements of the things of this world; the human spirit may be inclined to do evil or good, depending upon whether the individual follows right reason or selfish desires. While grace does not destroy nature but perfects and supernaturalizes it, the devil utilizes human weakness and the effects of original sin to further his evil aims."

In his book *Spiritual Theology,* Rev. Aumann, OP also indicated that as discernment of the spirit is necessary, one must be able to differentiate the types of spirit that influence us. The types of spirit are:

A. Divine Spirit

The following are the characteristics of Divine Spirit:

1. "Truth: God is truth and can not inspire anything but truth in a soul. Therefore, if a person believed to be inspired by God maintains opinions that are manifestly against revealed truth, the infallible teaching of the Church, or proven theology or philosophy or science, it must be concluded that the individual is deluded by the devil or is the victim of excessive imagination or faulty reasoning.
2. Gravity: God is never the cause of the things that are useless, futile, frivolous, or impertinent. When His spirit moves a soul, it is for something serious and beneficial.
3. Enlightenment: Although one may not always understand the meaning of an inspiration from God, the effect of any divine movement or impulse is always enlightenment and certitude rather than darkness

and confusion. This is true for both the effects on the individual who receives the inspiration and its effects on others.

4. Docility: Souls that are moved by the spirit of God accept cheerfully the advice and counsel of their directors or others who have authority over them. The spirit of obedience, docility, and submission is one of the clearest signs that a particular inspiration or movement is from God. This is especially true in case of the educated, who have greater tendency to be attached to their opinions.

5. Discretion: The spirit of God makes the soul discreet, prudent, and thoughtful in all actions. There is nothing of precipitation, lightness, exaggeration, or impetuosity; all is well balanced, edifying, serious, and full of calmness and peace.

6. Humility: The Holy Spirit always fills the soul with sentiments of humility and self-effacement. The loftier the communications from on high, the more profoundly the soul recognizes the abyss of its own nothingness. Mary said, "I am the servant of the Lord. Let it done to me as you say" (Luke 1:38).

7. Peace: St. Paul speaks frequently of the peace that comes from God (Rom. 15:33, Phil. 4:9), and Jesus mentions peace as one of the manifestations of his spirit (John 14:27). This is a quality that always accompanies communications from God; the soul experiences a profound and stable serenity in the depths of the spirit.

8. Confidence in God: This is a counterpart to and necessary consequence of true humility. Recognizing that of itself it can do nothing, as St. Paul says, "The soul throws itself on the power and mercy of God with a child like trust. Then it learns that it can do all things in Him" (Phil. 4:13).

9. Flexibility of Will: This sign consists primarily in a certain promptness of the will to subject itself to the inspirations and invitations of God. Secondarily, it consists of a facility in following the advice and counsel of others, especially if they are superiors, confessors, or spiritual directors. It is opposed to the rigid and unyielding will that is characteristic of those who are filled with self-love.

10. Purity of intention: The soul seeks only the glory of God in all it does and the perfect fulfillment of the will of God, without human interest or motivation out of self-love.

11. Patience in suffering: Suffering is frequently the best touchstone for revealing the true worth of an individual. No matter what the source of

the suffering, or whether it is just received or not, the soul bears it with patience and equanimity and uses it as a means of further perfection.

12. Self-abnegation: The words of Christ Himself are sufficient evidence that this is a sign of the spirit of God: "If anyone wants to be a follower of mine, let him renounce himself and take up his cross and follow me." (Matthew 16:24)

13. Simplicity: Together with veracity and sincerity, this characteristic is never lacking in those who are truly motivated by the spirit of God. Any duplicity, arrogance, hypocrisy, or vanity must be attributed rather to the spirit of the devil, the father of lies.

14. Liberty of spirit: First of all, there is no attachment to any created thing, not even to the gifts received from God. Secondly, all is accepted from the hands of God with gratitude and humility, whether it be a question of consolation or trial. Thirdly, while all duties and spiritual exercises are performed with promptness and punctuality, the soul is ready to leave even the most consoling and profitable exercise as soon as the charity of God calls it elsewhere. Liberty in spirit enables the soul to live in a state of constant joy and eagerness for the things of God.

15. Desire to imitate Christ: St. Paul says that it is impossible to have spirit of God without the spirit of Christ. (Romans 8:9). It is for this reason St. John of the Cross states that the soul that aspires to perfection must have a desire to imitate Christ in all things by conforming its life as much as possible to His." (J. Aumann, 1987, pp. 1-5)

B. Human Spirit

If we respond to grace, then we are able to rise above the temptations present before us. Otherwise, the human spirit is weak, vulnerable to the allures of the world, easily susceptible to self-centeredness, and in search of comfort and pleasure.

According to Rev. Aumann, it is sometimes difficult in practice to judge whether given manifestations proceed from the devil or from a purely human and egoistic spirit, but it is always relatively easy to distinguish between these two and the spirit of God. It will be possible in most cases, therefore, to determine that a given spirit could not possibly be from God and that it must be combated, even if one is not sure whether it is in fact from the devil or the human ego. The following contrasts may serve as general rules for distinguishing between diabolical and the human spirit.

Natural impulses and inclinations are spontaneous; they can be naturally traced to some natural cause or disposition; the stimulation of the senses acts upon, the interior powers, and they often persist in spite of prayer.

Diabolical impulse, on the other hand, is usually violent and difficult to prevent; it arises unexpectedly or with the slightest provocation; a mental suggestion excites the senses and disappears as a rule with prayer. Self-denial and rectitude of intention are excellent remedies against the spirit of egoism.

(J. Aumann, 1987, pp. 1-5)

C. Diabolical Spirit

The most common attack on a daily basis for most people is temptation, the enticement to choose something evil or sinful. However, the more serious types of attacks will be described later under the Diabolical Assessment section.

Before any interview, a clinician is encouraged to pray. Every clinician must start the day in prayer. In addition, prior to meeting any patient that was referred for ruling out a diabolical problem, prayer and fasting are recommended. The clinician who is in the state of grace becomes a living vessel through which grace can flow. God works through people. The clinician may be an instrument of God to determine what kind of condition is present in the client. With the help of the Holy Spirit, the clinician is able to sense something is visibly wrong by the mere presence of the client. A holy person, like Blessed Pope John Paul II or Blessed Mother Teresa of Calcutta, radiated the light of God in their very being. People are drawn like magnets to their holy presence and they long for their touch, even to the point of evoking tears. The same is true with evil. The very presence of the patient with a diabolical problem presents an evil presence. There is an internal repulsion away from such an individual. However, since every person is a child of God, the client is to be treated with respect and dignity. The interview takes place just like any other interview of a client coming to the office. In addition though, a number of questions are raised to determine the exposure of this client to anything that may have served as a door for the evil one to enter.

VULNERABILITY TO EVIL ATTACKS

A mother brought in a nine-year-old daughter who was extremely defiant and violent. The child was home schooled so the mother had an opportunity to observe the child's behavior all day. What was most disturbing to the mother was the way the child urinated and defecated everywhere in the house and smeared the walls with disgusting presence of feces. No matter what disciplinary action was taken, the child did not change. Upon entering the room for the interview, the child was suspicious and guarded. She refused to be seen. As I tried to make the child comfortable, she started speaking in a low, elderly guttural voice of a man threatening me to leave her alone. The child behaved erratically and uncontrollably. As I ensured the safety of the child in another room, I asked the mother what significant history she could share to shed light to this child's bizarre behavior. The mother confessed that she has limited history since her daughter was adopted and there was little known of this abandoned child.

Past family history could reveal exposure to things that a child or an adult may or may not have intentionally desired to welcome evil, but opened the doors to the occult. The following questions are worthwhile asking so that as a clinician, one has the chance to see the interconnection of delving into the occult with diabolical conditions. Being forewarned is also being forearmed. The mental health professional will be armed with proper information to share with the clergy during the referral. For future research, the data collected could be very valuable. Instead of simple observations, we can gather sufficient information to produce statistically significant information. The following questions may be asked:

Have you or someone in your family-

- Played with Ouija board?
- Played Dungeons and Dragons©, Magic the Gathering© cards, or other occult games?
- Consulted a psychic?

- Sought the help of a channeler, spiritist, or medium?
- Participated in witchcraft or associated with witches?
- Got involved in a black mass or devil worship?
- Joined Free Masonry and other such secret clubs?
- Made an oath to an anti-God organization?
- Consulted a palm reader?
- Believed in horoscopes or astrology?
- Consulted a tarot card reader?
- Enjoyed reading books, magazines or watching materials on TV, movies or playing video games with horror, occultic thriller, diabolical, or extremely violent themes?
- Been involved in satanic or voodoo activities?
- Collected or used charms and crystals believed to have powers?
- Been involved in crystal gazing?
- Kept in the house ancient or collectible items used by other cultures for pagan worship or associated with deities?
- Associated with those who wear gothic clothing, listen to heavy metal music, or prefer dark, violent, or immoral lyrics in music?
- Participated in healing services invoking the devil?
- Been obsessed or fascinated with magical, diabolical, or unexplainable phenomenon associated with the dark side?
- Been attracted to anything forbidden and evil in defiance of social norms?
- Used the internet, telephone, or TV for evil purposes?
- Lived in a house where the previous residents were involved in the occult or where something bad or tragic happened in that place?

The above scenarios are simply examples of situations wherein evil may come into a person or family. The extent of vulnerability varies with each individual, depending on the strength or weakness of the individual and the number of extenuating circumstances that opened the doors for that person or family. One must confer with a member of the clergy if any of these findings is unearthed.

It is noteworthy to comment that a patient may have a psychological condition and a diabolical condition simultaneously. This makes assessment even more complicated as one delineates what is psychological and what is diabolical. Since many signs and symptoms may overlap, the clinician's role is to use one's clinical judgment to determine and address the psycho-physiological problems in order to reduce those signs and symptoms. The appropriate therapeutic regimen needs to be applied to evaluate their effectiveness. The value of addressing the psycho-physiological problems first is to find out to what extent the presenting problems are alleviated before going any further. As I mentioned earlier in ruling out conditions, I consider the diabolical as the last possibility when everything else has been ruled out. The only exception that may occur that requires immediate attention is when a diabolical possession presents itself. One has to act immediately since a member of the clergy is needed.

Appendix D contains the specific signs and symptoms associated with the four levels of diabolical attacks. It is important to keep in mind that the data to be collected from these questionnaires, meaning both the diabolical exposure and the diabolical assessment, can be used for future research in order to establish a standardized diabolical interview questionnaire valuable to clinical practice. Every clinician who happens to run into such unusual conditions will have a diagnostic instrument available for his use and can independently go over the list to help differentiate one condition from another. The listed signs and symptoms are not meant to be a complete listing, but a reflection of the most commonly reported signs and symptoms of my patients.

DIABOLICAL ASSESSMENT

Every clinician is called to make a judgment as to what is going on with the referred client. As mentioned earlier, proper discernment is necessary in order to delineate the type of condition the patient is experiencing, as each condition requires a different approach. The following are a listing of the most common manifestations of diabolical conditions. The best way to explain the differences in each condition is to compare the degree of diabolical attack to a visible attack represented by insects called ticks. The eastern United States has an epidemic problem with a particular species of tick, *Ixodes scapularis,* which can transmit a bacterial infection leading to a chronic condition called Lyme disease. An area may be **infested** with ticks, which can be compared to **diabolical infestation**, the lowest level of attack. If the tick or ticks **attacked** and **adhered** to the skin of a person, this can be compared to **diabolical**

oppression, meaning the attack is on the outside. There is a problem, but the enemy is only on the periphery. If the infected tick managed to lodge itself for an extended period and the bacteria **entered the body,** spirochete bacterium will create problems in the areas of the body where the bacteria are present. This can be compared to **diabolical obsession** since there is infiltration of the body. If Lyme disease **spreads throughout the body** causing systemic failure, then this can be compared to **diabolical possession,** the extreme form of attack from the evil one.

SCHEMATIC DRAWINGS OF DIABOLICAL ATTACKS

INFESTATION

OPPRESSION

Level 1

Evil presence in the
environment

Level 2

Evil attacks the person
from the outside

OBSESSION

POSSESSION

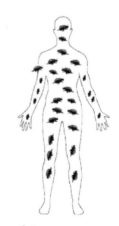

Level 3

Evil partially infiltrates
the human mind and body

Level 4

Evil totally infiltrates the
human mind and body

DIABOLICAL INFESTATION

Infestation is the unexplainable evil presence in a particular location, object, or other living beings, like animals, insects, etc., simply noted by the observer, but not directed to that person.

- Things fly, shake, rattle, or move unexplainably
- Inexplicable movements in a room or house that gives an eerie, "spooky" feeling
- Peculiar smells or sounds, an evil presence in a place, or the grounds seem to be disturbed
- Objects seem inhabited by unexplainable forces, considered eerie and evil
- Equipment may turn on and off or may act peculiarly
- Weird, scary behavior of animals uncharacteristic behavior of that breed
- Unusual and unexplained activities in a closet or room, e.g., lights flickering on or off

Evil is real and not to be taken lightly. Scott Peck, MD, for example, did not believe in the reality of the devil until he encountered possession cases in his practice. In Chapter 5 of his book *People of the Lie,* he acknowledged that 99% of psychiatrists did not believe in evil spirit.

> "Of course, I did not believe that possession existed. In fifteen years of busy psychiatric practice, I had never seen anything faintly resembling a case.[. . .] So I decided to go out and look for a case. I wrote around and let it be known that I was interested in observing cases of purported possession for evaluation. Referrals trickled in [. . .]. These two were highly unusual in that both these cases are of satanic possession. I know now that Satan is real. I have met it. Each case was extraordinarily complex-far more than usual psychiatric patients [. . .]. The skeptical reader is likely to ask, "How can you hope to prove to me the reality of the devil when you don't even present your evidence?" The answer is that I don't hope to convince the reader of Satan's reality. Conversion to a belief in God generally requires some kind of actual encounter—a personal

experience—with the living God. Conversion to a belief in Satan is no different." (S. Peck, 1983, pp. 182-184)

However, even C.S. Lewis managed to present the reality of evil in a clever, satirical form in his book "The Screwtape Letters." In one of the letters a seasoned devil, Screwtape, writes to his apprentice and nephew, Wormwood, an amateur devil, as presented here.

"My dear Wormwood,

The real trouble about the set of your patient is living in is that it is merely Christian. They all have individual interests, of course, but the bond remains mere Christianity. What we want, if men become Christians at all, is to keep them in the state of mind I call 'Christianity And.' You know—Christianity and the Crisis, Christianity and the New Psychology, Christianity and the New Order, Christianity and Faith Healing, Christianity and Psychical Research, Christianity and Vegetarianism, Christianity and Spelling Reform. If they must be Christians, let them at least be Christians with a difference. Substitute for the faith itself some Fashion with a Christian colouring. Work on their horror of the same Old Thing.

The horror of the Same Old Thing is one of the most valuable passions we have produced in the human heart—an endless source of heresies in religion, folly in counsel, infidelity in marriage, and inconstancy in friendship. The humans live in time, and experience reality successively. To experience much of it, therefore, they must experience many different things. In other words, they must experience change. And since they need change, the Enemy (being a hedonist at heart) has made change pleasurable to them. But he does not wish them to make change, any more than eating, an end in itself, He has balanced the love of change in them by a love of permanence which we call Rhythm. He gives them the seasons, each season different yet every year the same, so that spring is always felt as a novelty yet always as the recurrence of an immemorial theme. He gives them in His Church, a spiritual year; they change from a fast to a feast, but it is the same feast as before.

Now just as we pick out and exaggerate the pleasure of eating to produce gluttony, so we pick out this natural pleasantness of change and twist it into a demand for absolute novelty. This demand is entirely our workmanship. If we neglect our duty, men will not only be contented but transported by the mix novelty and familiarity of snowdrops this January, sunrise this morning, plum pudding this Christmas. Children, until we have taught them better, will be perfectly happy with a seasonal round of games in which conkers succeed hopscotch as regularly as autumn follows summer. Only by our incessant efforts is the demand for infinite, or unrhythmical, change kept up.

This demand is valuable in various ways. In the first place it diminishes pleasure while increasing desire. The pleasure of novelty is by its very nature more subject than any other to the law of diminishing returns. And continued novelty costs money, so the desire for it spells avarice or unhappiness or both. And again, the more rapacious this desire, the sooner it must eat up all the innocent sources of pleasure and pass on to those the Enemy forbids. Thus by inflaming the horror of the same Old Thing, we have recently made the Arts, for example, less dangerous to us than, perhaps, they have ever been, "lowbrow" and "highbrow" artists alike being now daily drawn into fresh, and still fresh, excesses of lasciviousness, unreason, cruelty, and pride. Finally, the desire for novelty is indispensible if we are to produce Fashions or Vogues.

The use of Fashions in thought is to distract the attention of men from their real dangers. We direct the fashionable outcry of each generation against those vices of which it is least in danger and fix its approval on the virtue nearest to that vice which we are trying to make endemic. The game is to have them all running about with fire extinguishers whenever there is flood, and all crowding to that side of the boat which is already nearly gunwale under. Thus we make it fashionable to expose the dangers of enthusiasm at the very moment when they are really becoming worldly and lukewarm; a century later when we are really making them all Byronic and drunk with emotion, the fashionable outcry is directed against the dangers of the mere "understanding." Cruel ages are put on their guard against sentimentality, feckless and idle ones Respectability, lecherous ones against Puritanism; and whenever all men are really hastening to be slaves or tyrants we make Liberalism the prime bogey.

But the greatest triumph of all is to elevate this horror of the same Old Thing into a philosophy so that nonsense in the intellect may reinforce corruption in the will. It is here that the general Evolutionary or Historical character of modern European thought (partly our work) comes in so usefully. The Enemy loves platitudes. Of a proposed course of action He wants men, so far as I can see, to ask very simple questions: Is it righteous? Is it prudent? Is it possible? Now if we can keep men asking: "Is it in accordance with the general movement of our time? Is it progressive or reactionary? Is this the way that History is going? They will neglect the relevant questions. And the questions they do ask are, of course, unanswerable; for they do not know the future and what the future will be depends largely on just those choices which they now invoke the future to help them to make. As a result, while their minds are buzzing in this vacuum, we have the better chance to slip in and bend them to the action we have decided on. And great work has already been done. Once they knew that some changes were for the better, and others for the worse, and others again indifferent. We have largely removed this knowledge. For the descriptive adjective "unchanged" we have substituted the emotional adjective "stagnant." We have trained them to think of the future as a promised land which favored heroes attain—not as something which everyone reaches at the rate of sixty minutes an hour, whatever he does, whoever he is.

Your affectionate uncle, SCREWTAPE (C.S. Lewis, 1942, pp. 126-130)

Let us reflect seriously on the message given by this satire which applies aptly to this present age. In fact, we can think of so many applications of these scenarios, so much so, it is likely that many have fallen into the traps laid out cunningly by the enemy, leading to a deeper involvement with their evil choices, and unknowingly leading them into the hands of the enemy.

DIABOLICAL OPPRESSION

Oppression consists of unexplainable direct attacks by "blocking" the person and those associated with the person. The attacks are outside the person to intimidate the individual.

- Frequent unexplained obstacles in life
- Feeling physically blocked by some forces outside the control of the individual
- Under frequent attack in family, finance, relationships, school work, or job by unexplainable forces
- Heavy feeling of an evil presence pressing on or pinning down the individual
- Feeling physically attacked by unseen enemies preventing the person from doing things
- Strange experience of often losing spiritually related items important to that person or to be used by that person
- Direct external physical attacks on the individual, such as tripping, falling, or being pushed down the stairs or blows leaving marks on the skin of unexplainable bruises and pain from unseen attackers
- Attack on the surrounding environment of the individual to harass the person, e.g. things are flying, moving to disturb the person, or equipment needed does not work

DIABOLICAL OBSESSION

Obsession is a two-pronged attack: one on the mind by relentless, harassing persecutory, vile, scrupulous, blasphemous, evil thoughts; and an attack from inside the person with partial infiltration of the human body. The highest level can be termed "partial possession." This can include:

- Being tormented by unrelenting and uncontrollable evil thoughts, music, and voices usually demonic in theme
- Extreme preoccupation with demonic ideas
- Extreme, persistent, and bizarre display of religiosity, but not to the point of psychosis
- Being tormented by hearing eerie and inexplicable disturbing noises

- Direct attack on the internal organs of the individual by the devil
- Diabolical visions and images to invoke fear in the person
- Unexplained physical illness not responding to any medical intervention
- Sexual stimulation and feeling of penetration by unseen evil forces
- Other attacks on the senses (e.g., a peculiar disgusting taste, obnoxious nauseating smell)

DIABOLICAL POSSESSION

Possession is a condition when the individual is fully taken over by evil spirit and has no control over bodily and cognitive functions. Some of the signs are:

- Evil has completely taken over a person against his will
- Involuntary movements propelled by forces outside the control of the individual
- Irrational behavior viewed by others as bizarre and evil, not responding to medical interventions
- Eyes are darting uncontrollably from side to side then rolled up completely with mostly white part (sclera) of the eyes being prominent with an evil presence
- Voice changing with eerie shrieking, a deep tone, or guttural, animalistic sounds, or hissing sound of a snake
- Able to predict or know hidden events that normally should not be known by the person
- Vile, profane, vulgar, blasphemous language
- Destruction of holy objects or sacred images
- Disrespect towards or withdrawal from religious people
- Extreme superhuman strength unexplainable despite the size of the individual
- Speaking in strange tongues and understanding strange language normally unfamiliar to the background of that individual
- Bizarre, uncharacteristic rituals against the person's will
- Supernatural power to spin, fly, or move against nature
- Body arches rigidly with hands forming like claws
- Aversion towards or spitting at the presence of the Holy Eucharist
- Reacting violently to the words: "In the name of Jesus Christ . . ."

CLINICAL COMPARISONS OF PSYCHOLOGICAL DISEASES FROM DIABOLICAL DISORDERS

"If any of you lacks wisdom, let him ask God, who gives to all men generously and without reproaching, and it will be given him."

—St. James

CHAPTER 5

CLINICAL COMPARISONS OF PSYCHOLOGICAL DISEASES FROM DIABOLICAL DISORDERS

The following chart is intended to be a guideline to help outline both the similarities of and differences between psychological and diabolical manifestations. This is not meant to be an exhaustive list of every possible sign; rather, it highlights the most common features seen in clinical practice. The observed signs and symptoms of the patient must be taken collectively, not singularly, since the entire picture of the presenting problem is what leads to the more definitive diagnosis. A clinician will observe that there are symptoms of mental illness that are similar to a diabolical case, but the latter arouses in a practitioner a foreboding feeling that one is dealing with supernatural forces beyond one's clinical expertise. When this happens, it is highly advisable to immediately seek a clergy if a possession is in front of the clinician or at least if one doubts the ability to handle the situation. In clinical practice, a patient may suffer from both a psychological disease while also undergoing diabolical attack. This is not unusual since the evil one takes advantage of the vulnerability of the mentally unstable patient. Such cases are inherently more complicated and challenging to treat.

PSYCHOTIC DEPRESSION	DIABOLICAL OPPRESSION
• Speech is incoherent and self-deprecatory	• Speech is coherent and relevant
• Speech content is focused on failings	• Speech content is focused on evil attacks
• Facies is downcast, dejected	• Facies is fearful, perplexed
• Crying, hopeless, helpless	• Mood is anxious, apprehensive
• Prefers to be alone	• Prefers to have the company of others for safety
• Positive family and/or personal history	• Does not necessarily have a previous history

PSYCHOTIC MANIA	DIABOLICAL POSSESSION
• Rapid, pressured speech	• Guttural noises, hissing or animalistic sounds different from the person's voice
• Can be violently aggressive	• Can be violently aggressive
• Hyperactivity	• Movements propelled by forces outside the control of the individual
• Intense, glaring, exophthalmic eyes	• Darting eyes then pupils fixate at the top, mostly showing sclera
• Unpredictable behavior	• Unpredictable behavior
• No physical contortions	• Body contorts; hands may form like claws; facial contortions
• Extremely strong	• May defy gravity or spin around without control with superhuman strength
• Erratically destructive	• Destructive towards religious objects

OBSESSIVE-COMPULSIVE DISORDER	DIABOLICAL OPPRESSION
• Bizarre, time-consuming rituals compelled by thoughts	• Frequent turn to prayer, which can become ritualistic
• Meaningless, repetitive movements	• Physically held down/shaken by unseen forces; unable to move
• Repetitive thoughts on the same issue associated with one's fears and anxieties	• Thoughts focused on peculiar diabolical attacks
• Annoying habits and compulsions	• No compulsions
• No physical attacks	• Unexplainable, unwelcomed, repetitive physical attacks by unseen forces
• No complaints about feeling a presence of evil	• Feeling a heavy presence of evil around the individual
• Feeling guilty if unable to do rituals	• Uncomfortable and does not want attacks; more frustration

PSYCHOLOGICAL OBSESSION	DIABOLICAL OBSESSION
• Persistent, tormenting thoughts on the same issue	• Persistent, tormenting thoughts on the same issue
• Excessive preoccupation with order; symmetry, sequencing of numbers	• No preoccupation with symmetry or order • Feeling of disorder, no control
• Preoccupation with cleanliness or contamination	• Not necessarily preoccupied with cleanliness or contamination
• Can be tormented by repetitive music and sounds	• Unwelcome, tormenting music and sounds with an evil theme

• Tormenting thoughts of one's sins	• Tormenting thoughts of one's sins • Being tormented by evil ideas
• Preoccupation with perfection	• Feeling of imperfection and vulnerability due to evil attacks

SCHIZOPHRENIA	DIABOLICAL OBSESSION
• Hearing voices (hallucinations); these may be tormenting	• Hearing tormenting, evil voices, music and/or sounds
• Disordered thinking (delusions)	• Tormenting thoughts attacking the person; able to explain lucidly
• Weeping, laughing or enraged	• Mood is anxious, apprehensive
• Long-term, biochemical imbalance	• Identifiable start of attacks
• Intense, suspicious eyes	• Anxious, worried eyes
• Positive family history; genetic	• May or may not have family history of same condition
• Disorganized speech	• Coherent speech • Able to explain attacks
• Flat affect	• Anxious affect

SCHIZOPHRENIA	DIABOLICAL INFESTATION
• Visual hallucinations	• Presence of evil in surroundings as verified by others
• Suspicious about surroundings	• Eerie images as verified by others
• Olfactory hallucinations	• Verifiable foul and eerie smells in the area

• Refusal to go anywhere due to paranoia	• Prefers not to be in the haunted room or house confirmed by others
• Auditory hallucinations	• Audible and eerie sounds in the area
• Suspicious about animals	• Weird behavior of animals as observed by others
• Suspicious about objects and people	• Unusual evil presence in objects as seen by others

DISSOCIATIVE IDENTITY DISORDER	DIABOLICAL POSSESSION
• Distinct personalities and corresponding identities	• Same person, but an evil personality comes out
• Different identity, but the same voice (may change inflection from regressive child-like quality varying up to appropriate age level)	• Same person, but voice is changed to guttural, hissing or animalistic sounds or voice may be lower, deep tone or may sound older than the person's age level
• Personality suddenly changes due to severe stress or extreme relaxation	• Sudden change due to the desire of the evil one to manifest • Sense of "presence" of evil which is unexplainable, but unmistakable, intangible, and inescapable
• Irrational behavior due to trauma	• Bizarre behavior not controlled by the person, but by the evil one
• No change in presence of religious objects or individuals	• Strong aversion to religious objects or individuals

• Each personality serves an emotional need of the person	• Evil personality manifests to torture and control the person
• The eyes are anxious or detached	• The eyes are darting uncontrollably, then the pupils fixate at the top, showing mostly the sclera

DEPERSONALIZATION PERSONALITY DISORDER	DIABOLICAL OBSESSION
• Continuous or recurring feelings that one is an outside observer of one's thoughts, of one's body or parts of the body	• Aware that one is being tormented by unwelcomed evil thoughts; perceives that body is attacked within by evil forces
• Numbing of one's senses or responses to the world around	• Aware and sensitive to one's senses and environment as affected by the evil one
• Feeling like a robot or like one is living in a dream or a movie	• Wishing the condition is just a dream
• The sensation that one is out of touch with self, as if an illusion	• The person is not in control, but the evil one is partly controlling the person
• The sense that one's body, legs or arms appear distorted, enlarged or shrunken	• The person complains that one is afflicted by the evil one in certain parts of the body

IN SUMMARY

PSYCHOTIC (Psychological)	DIABOLICAL (Possession)
P—psychotic or flat affect	D—demonic theme in thought, speech, and behavior
S—suspicious and delusional	I—irrationally vile, blasphemous speech
Y—yelling, glaring eyes	A—abnormally darting eyes then fixated upwards
C—confused and grossly erratic behavior	B—bizarre, foreboding demonic behavior with bodily contortions
H—hallucinations	O—ominous, repulsive reaction against holy objects, religious people, and the holy name of Jesus Christ
O—out of touch with reality	L—lowered, guttural, animalistic, eerie, inhuman sounds coming from the person
T—threatening, dangerous behavior	I—intangible, invisible, inescapable presence of evil that is unexplainable
I—irrational, incoherent speech	C—chilly, dropping of room temperature which may or may not be accompanied by a peculiar stench
C—confusion, disorientation	A—aware of hidden information or able to predict events
	L—levitations, supernatural strength, able to move against forces of nature

CASE STUDIES

"Think well. Speak well. Do well. These three things, through the mercy of God, will make a man go to Heaven."

—St. Camillus de Lellis

CHAPTER 6

IS IT DIABOLICAL POSSESSION
OR A PSYCHOTIC EPISODE?

CASE A

A 39-year-old, married, female patient was referred by her primary care physician for psychological evaluation. She has been claiming to have invisible stigmata causing her pain. Instead of mystical manifestations, the patient displayed signs of a diabolical condition. She also has a history of psychiatric problems with a diagnosis of bipolar and borderline personality disorder. The enclosed history includes the review of medical records and interview with her psychiatrist, counselor, husband and priests.

PRESENTING PROBLEMS:

Over the phone, the patient complained that she was experiencing extreme burning pain from her invisible stigmata in both hands, feet, and around her head, and receiving inner locutions and visions from our Lord Jesus Christ, the Blessed Virgin Mary, and the saints. She claimed to have had the stigmata for a few years and that she was a victim soul.

She came to the office with disheveled hair, multiple tattoos, and clad in a very short skirt and a tank top that bared her midriff. She looked confused and struggled to walk because she was so unsteady on her feet. Upon entering the room, her eyes rolled up and she lowered her head. As an evil look spread across her face, a voice came from within her that was a gruff, animalistic, guttural, growling sound, which said, "We don't want to be here." She was fighting with somebody and her face was contorting. Her body stiffened, her arms and hands were like claws, her back arched, and her head moved very fast. She was thrashing her body and slid down the recliner.

MEDICAL HISTORY:

Her birth history was uneventful. Her early childhood and adolescent years were uneventful. She was a relatively healthy adult with two previous surgeries.

EDUCATIONAL HISTORY:

At an early age, she was diagnosed with a learning disability. She had attention deficit with hyperactivity and dyslexia. In school, though she was put in special education classes, she continued to have difficulties to the point of failing, and was made fun of by her classmates. She received a Catholic education from elementary through high school, but sadly received terrible treatment.

FAMILY HISTORY:

She was the oldest of ten children. As for the family history, she described her father as someone with a bad temper and anger issues, who was emotionally unavailable and moody, who could vacillate quickly between happy and mad. Her brothers suffered from depression and ADHD and felt rejected by their father and unwanted. There were multiple psychiatric problems on the father's side of the family. The paternal grandfather was an alcoholic and suffered from depression. The paternal grandmother suffered from depression. A paternal aunt was hospitalized for mental illness. Her father's sister suffered from depression.

She was married with four elementary-aged daughters who seemed to be doing well and studying in a Catholic school.

PSYCHOLOGICAL HISTORY:

She did not respond to her environment like her peers of the same age. She rocked herself in a corner and banged her head against the wall and had periods of rage. At age five, she was easily confused and her responses were not appropriate. She did not understand what people were saying and she had difficulty expressing herself. Instead of being sad about a given situation, she would laugh. As a teenager, she had periods of depression. She felt rejected and was teased by other children. She felt abandoned and alone. She was emotionally immature. She had mental health problems all her life and described herself as two different people: a happy, fun person and a mean, argumentative, vicious one. As a child, she had been sexually molested by a baby-sitter and a relative. She started abusing alcohol to make up for her loneliness and feelings of depression. She started cutting herself superficially. It was not until the birth of her children that she showed signs of a more serious biochemical imbalance and was given medication to stabilize her mood swings. She called herself a "rapid cycler," having manic and depressive episodes frequently.

SPIRITUAL HISTORY:

She was a baptized and was raised a practicing Catholic. There was a period as a young adult in which she was not practicing her faith. She got involved with other young people who played with tarot cards and an Ouija board. She moved in with her boyfriend, then married him civilly. She stopped going to church. She said the evil manifestations became obvious then, but she had a conversion and returned to the church in her 30s. At this point, she claimed to have started having mystical experiences, offered herself to Christ as a victim soul, and was mystically married to Christ. She claimed to have private revelations given to her by Jesus Christ.

A few months earlier, she experienced profuse spiritual attacks. She thought that Christ was asking her to suffer for souls. She expressed her love for God and her willingness to suffer but was scared of the consequences of this offering. She turned to the Blessed Mother for comfort and discernment. She was assured that her husband would be converted and to trust in the Lord. Her husband was from a family that did not practice any religion so, as an adult, he did not believe in God and had no belief in the presence of a soul. It was stressful for the wife to discuss anything spiritual with her husband because they were so far apart in their beliefs and he did not understand anything religious she tried to discuss with him. She physically hid in the closet and talked to her mother's and priests' friends, but also hid her diabolical attacks from her family by staying in the closet. She had collected a number of horror films and enjoyed viewing them constantly to the point of being obsessed with them as observed by the husband. Her mother expressed concern about her daughter's preoccupation with horror films, stating, "She is inviting in whatever it is. She is letting it happen." She continued to share that her daughter researched the different saints then tried to become extremely preoccupied with whatever saint on which she was focusing that week, identifying herself with that particular saint. In the same breath, she talked about demons frequently. She had bizarre, religiously preoccupied thoughts. She claimed to have had mystical experiences right there in front of me during our therapy sessions, but her eyes looked sad, anxious and fearful. She asked if I saw the presence of our Lord Jesus Christ or the Blessed Virgin Mary in the room or if I could smell roses, but I experienced no such thing. She appeared to be in pain when she crossed her hands and stiffened her arms, expressing that she had pain in her hands. She crossed her feet and straightened them as she complained of pain in her feet. She told me that she had invisible stigmata that she claimed was part of her role as a suffering soul for Christ. It was hard to believe her statement since she appeared to be distraught rather than resigned.

In four successive sessions, she came into the room struggling and fighting to take control of herself against the evil forces that took over her. She extended her tongue and started panting, then her head would thrash back and forth with her eyes rolled up and her face contorted. Sounds of hissing, like a snake and a low, guttural, masculine sound came out of her mouth. She was able to overcome evil as we prayed and used the holy water generously. She calmed down and felt consoled by the saints. She always came out of the manifestations crying, embarrassed, and wondering how long she had to suffer this way. She was seeing an evil, green dragon and evil forces in the room and complained that a green, hairy, ugly animal was attacking her soul. During one of her later visits, I brought a relic of the True Cross. She noticed it as soon as she entered the room. Surprisingly, she did not have any manifestations and we were actually able to have a full session. She brought all kinds of religious objects and pictures in magazines that she had cut out, which reflected her various moods.

She responded with ratings of seven to ten on a scale of 0-10, with ten being the worst for the following Diabolical Assessment questions:

- Evil has taken over against her will
- Involuntary movements of her body and extremities propelled by outside forces
- Irrational behavior viewed by others as scary
- Voice changed with eerie, evil tone against person's will
- Vile, profane, vulgar, blasphemous angry language
- Destruction of sacred images or holy objects
- Extreme, extraordinary strength
- Enraged, cursing God
- Evil eyes, evil expression and demeanor
- Aversion to the Holy Eucharist
- Unexplained obstacles and being blocked in doing things
- Heavy feeling of an evil presence within the person
- Evil attacking this person
- Medical treatments do not change the problems
- Tormented by unrelenting, uncontrollable evil thoughts
- Evil presence surrounding the person
- Seeing evil presence in visible forms, images
- Eerie unexplained noises
- Peculiar smell, sound, or evil presence around her

She shared with me all her journals that were contained in a large plastic bin. There were distinct differences in her regular penmanship compared to her writings and drawings, which contained evil content and images. Her voluminous writings revealed extreme religious themes of communication with God and the saints.

CLINICAL DIAGNOSIS:

She responded to the Bipolar Questionnaire with ratings of eight to ten on a scale of 0 to 10 with 10 being worst on the following items:

- Rapid, pressured speech
- Full of energy with little rest
- Impatient
- Spending too much
- Extreme strength

- Reckless behavior, pushing limits
- Mood swings
- Enraged
- Helplessness, hopelessness
- Sleeping all the time when depressed
- Overwhelming unhappiness
- Lack of appetite when depressed
- Low self-esteem
- Fatigued
- Prefers to be alone and does not want to talk
- Tearful, crying with no provocation
- Diminished interest
- Suicidal ideas, but will not act on them

She was diagnosed by her previous psychiatrist to have concurrent borderline personality disorder as an adult. The following are some of her signs and symptoms:

- Intense fear of abandonment; fearful of rejection
- Unstable self-image or sense of identity
- Impulsive and self-destructive behaviors
- Suicidal behavior (suicidal attempt) or self-injury (self-cutting)
- Wide mood swings
- Chronic feelings of emptiness
- Anger-related problems, such as frequently losing temper
- Periods of paranoia and loss of contact with reality

She completed some questionnaires. Her Symptoms Checklist showed headaches, irritability, poor concentration and feeling sick. Her Hamilton Anxiety Scales revealed mild anxiety, but her behavior showed evidence of a higher level of anxiety. Her Beck's Depression scale showed mild depression. Stress Audit revealed elevated family stressors. Her Mental Status Exam revealed an age-appropriate appearance, seductive and revealing tight clothing, and behavior that was bizarre for half of the session (during diabolical manifestation); otherwise, her demeanor fluctuated from somber to joyful, from giggly to rapid, pressured speech. At times, she was agitated, hyperactive, tearful, labile, anxious, and mildly depressed. She remarked about being easily distracted with difficulty concentrating. She was oriented to time, place, and person. She was able to recall events but she struggled with timeframes, needing to correct her earlier statements. Her thought content showed a religious and delusional preoccupation. She has described visual, olfactory, and auditory hallucinations that actually were a part of her diabolical manifestations, that is, evil mimicking and presenting itself as good. The anti-psychotic medication had not altered her signs and symptoms because evil had taken over her. Evil tried to hide by manifesting as pain in the extremities which the patient identified as stigmata and sharing certain revelations through her that were already typically known. The person was prayed over (deliverance prayers) for a number of hours and the person became normal. The mystical experiences were associated with the diabolical possession. The psychiatrist continued to treat the patient.

CASE B

A 55-year-old patient came to see me to receive assistance with her perceived diabolical problems described as consistent, daily attacks. She wanted to convince more people of her mystical experiences and that the devil had possessed her. The following assessment was a result of the interview with her psychologist, husband, spiritual director, and friend.

PRESENTING PROBLEMS:

She complained about hearing eerie sounds and loud screams; animal-like guttural sounds coming out from her mouth; and experiencing facial contortions that happened against her will. She claimed that she had the presence of evil within her. These problems occurred after she offered herself to God for the sufferings of her family members. Several years prior, she felt a diabolical take-over and the evil one entered her. She felt weird and started saying things like "Out!" Her head moved quickly. She could smell something burning in the closet so she used holy water since she felt the heavy presence of evil.

MEDICAL HISTORY:

She appeared to be a healthy adult female who was not currently taking any prescription medications or any vitamins. She used to smoke cigarettes, which she stopped 20 years ago. She also tried marijuana and cocaine as a teenager to self-medicate. She used to abuse alcohol as a young adult, but she stopped after college.

FAMILY HISTORY:

Her family had a positive history of depression, bipolar, and anxiety disorder. Her parents were divorced and her mother re-married five times. Her mother was mentally abusive, leading to conflict and an emotional disconnect with her. Her father abused alcohol and died of liver failure. She was an only child. She was married with only one child.

PSYCHOLOGICAL HISTORY:

She was admitted at the hospital for her unusual behavior that frightened her husband, who found her submerged in holy water in the bathtub surrounded by all kinds of religious objects and lighted candles in order to ward off evil spirits attacking her. She was screaming and "crazy things" were coming out of her mouth. The incident was so bizarre that this required psychological evaluation. She claimed to have been spinning in circles and to have lain down on the cot with her body forming a cruciform pose, but there were no witnesses. While in the hospital, she lay awake at night holding on to a small crucifix and she was released after two days. She refused any medications given to her. After her discharge from the hospital, she was prayed over using exorcism prayers on several occasions, but nothing worked.

She saw a psychologist and the psychological testing revealed the following results:

MMPI-2: a woman who attempted to place herself overly in a positive light by minimizing faults and denying psychological problems. The defensive stance is characteristic of individuals who are trying to maintain the appearance of adequacy and self-control. This client tends to deny problems and is not very introspective or insightful about her own behavior. She omitted 10 items on the MMPI-2, though this was not enough to invalidate the results, but some of her scale scores were likely lower than expected because of these omissions.

Millon Clinical Multi-axial Inventory: A distinct tendency toward avoiding self-disclosure is evident in this patient's response. If denial tendencies are present, she may be covering up significant symptoms. She appears to fit the Axis II classifications best: Histrionic Personality Traits, Obsessive Compulsive Personality Features, and Narcissistic Personality Features. The psychologist had the following recommendations:

With therapeutic warmth and understanding, she may be able to maintain self-assurance and a posture of maturity, without viewing therapy as a threat to her self-image. Although she is concerned about appearances, such as being well thought of by a therapist, a supportive and cognitive reframing regimen may overcome her inclination to resist or deny psychological interpretations. Her defensiveness on these matters should be honored in any short-term therapeutic approach, and probing and insight should proceed at a careful pace. Once trust and confidence have developed in the relationship, however, cognitive methods may begin to be employed to supplant the patient's pretenses and cynicism with less defensive attitudes and behavior.

SPIRITUAL HISTORY:

She was baptized and raised as a Catholic. She was married civilly to her husband and was finally married in the Catholic church. She and her husband had a conversion at which point her husband entered the Catholic Church.

She felt that she was exposed to the occult through her mother who used Ouija board and tarot cards. She consulted a palm reader, believed in horoscopes, consulted a psychic, and listened to heavy metal music in her younger years. She believed that she was living in a diabolically infested home because a priest said to her that there was a presence of evil in her house. She described and claimed to have the following behavior:

- Claiming something evil took over against her will;
- Involuntary movements of her head forced by the evil one; facial contortions;
- Voice changing against her will; vile, profane, blasphemous language;
- Disrespect towards holy objects;
- Predicting the election of the Pope;
- Levitations of arms and legs;
- Aversion against a religious person;

- Unexplained physical discomfort; heavy feeling of evil presence within her; evil attacking her and no healing despite repeated prayer over;
- Attack on her marriage and finances;
- Claiming to be tormented by unrelenting evil thoughts;
- Evil presence around her; physically attacked by evil forces; weird scenarios surrounding her;
- She felt evil presence in the house and a peculiar smell in a closet.

CLINICAL DIAGNOSIS:

This is the case of a 55-year-old, married woman who was accompanied by a friend. She brought with her a thick binder to give a full history of her condition, explaining the events in her life in the past ten years and the people she sought for help. She was very anxious to share her life story. Her speech was pressured, rapid, emphatic, incoherent and at times irrelevant. Her eyes were glaringly intense with good eye contact. She was colorfully attired with excessive make-up. She often changed her position from sitting to standing. Her posture while standing was such that she stood two feet away from me and had one hand to her waist while the other hand was constantly gesturing. She was determined to get help for her diabolical condition. She produced the scuffing sound and moved her head very fast to the side to demonstrate to me that she was being controlled by something else. She expressed a strong desire to be holy and her willingness to be a sacrificial soul for others. She was active in the church ministries, faithful in her prayers, and regular in the reception of the holy sacraments. While we were praying, she moved forward quickly on her knees from the back to the front of us and lowered her head in prayer. She seemed to have a need for tremendous attention. As I reviewed her binder, she sought many priests and bishops to get help for her condition. She wrote numerous letters explaining her spiritual gifts and her diabolical attacks in attempts to obtain an exorcism. She seemed to be seeking approval and confirmation of her supernatural experiences from many priests. She did not suffer quietly, but often talked about her crosses. She was observed to be angry and defensive when she did not get the answer she was seeking. She often talked about obedience but her actions were the contrary, namely, she was pushing for what she wanted to happen. The interview with her husband, her psychologist, and her primary care physician did not reveal any observable mystical or diabolical phenomenon.

Her Assessment Form and Symptoms Checklist revealed a serious sleep disorder, that is, not sleeping for days, experiencing conflict with others, fatigue, dyspnea, speech difficulty, and urinary difficulty. She finally revealed having depression episodes in the past after further inquiry. Her Stress Audit revealed marital problems. The Bipolar Questionnaire checklist seemed to show a number of red flags verifying the diagnosis:

- her speech is rapid and pressured
- she talks so fast that she seemed to have racing thoughts
- she admitted not sleeping for one to four days or longer at times; she stayed very busy and productive while her family was asleep
- extremely energetic and hyperactive
- grandiose ideas with religious preoccupation that she has mystical experiences and levitation
- sense of entitlement
- extreme strength and showing others how she could lift an 80 lb concrete block
- moody and so unpredictable as to her mood
- not accepting her faults, blaming others for things happening; she was always correct
- periods of sadness and isolation in a dark room
- periods of overwhelming unhappiness; tearfulness
- periods of exhaustion after being in high gear, non-stop volunteer work and house work

The husband described her in the past five years as driven, obsessive, strong-willed, relentless, uncompromising, talking loudly and continuously making it hard to get words in, pushy, aggressive, unable to relax, constantly busy, going from one event to another, wearing herself out to the point of exhaustion, and eventually staying in her room in darkness. After a couple of days, she was back to her normal self. She has signs and symptoms of bipolar I with religious delusions. In listening to the description of her religious experiences, it seemed that she was having delusion and hallucinations perceived as mystical experiences and diabolical attacks. She completed a questionnaire about her temperament twice, but in both cases her responses were invalid since the person in my presence was a total opposite of whom she was projecting. She wanted to project a laid-back, easy-going, phlegmatic temperament. Her friend and her husband showed a more accurate description of an aggressive-persuasive personality. She had more a sanguine-choleric temperament. She always wanted to present herself again in the most favorable light.

I recommended for her to see a psychiatrist so she could start on medication for her condition. She refused to see one and demanded that her condition was spiritual. She stopped coming for further counseling.

CHAPTER 7

IS IT DIABOLICAL OBSESSION OR PSYCHOLOGICAL OBSESSION?

Case A

A 60-year-old, married man was complaining of needing to check and re-check things, needing to walk in a particular pattern, constantly counting as he did things, frequent hand washing, with many long rituals that he felt compelled to do, otherwise fears set in and he experienced tremendous anxiety.

PRESENTING PROBLEMS:

He recalled being a teenager when he noticed that he had to undo and re-do whatever he was doing. He took long showers and was fearful of using just any commode. He was even afraid that he might even cause a woman to get pregnant by simply using the same bathroom. Even though he knew it was ridiculous, he still could not help but thinking this way. Since that time, he suffered exaggerated fears. His initial fears were connected with his harsh father, who would not allow him to make mistakes. He had to do things perfectly or else he suffered severe punishment. The rigidity of his father influenced him to be strict with himself as well. His symptoms of obsessive-compulsive disorder (OCD) were at times crippling and routines took him longer.

MEDICAL HISTORY:

He was a very healthy young man and was used to hard work. He never smoked and never attempted any illicit drugs. Though he used to drink alcohol heavily, he decided to stop completely and had been sober for ten years. He had no allergies. He suffered from headaches, high blood pressure, and high cholesterol, for which his physician had prescribed him medications.

FAMILY HISTORY:

He was the oldest and the only boy with four sisters. He described his father as having serious anger problems and was very rigid. His mother was loving and attentive to him, but she suffered from depression. Bipolar disorder ran in his father's side of the family.

EDUCATIONAL HISTORY:

He wanted to get out of the house, so he immediately joined the military after high school. He completed college from his military educational benefits and paid for his other expenses to pursue his graduate studies in his area of interest. He then became a teacher.

PSYCHOLOGICAL HISTORY:

He was never taken for counseling as a young man because his father did not believe in it. It was considered a weakness and men were supposed to be strong, not weak. He finally was able to seek counseling as a grown man when his mother died, deeply grieving her death. He was left with a cruel, demeaning father who was physically and emotionally abusive towards him when he was a little boy. He continued with psychotherapy, even marital therapy with his wife. He was prescribed paroxetine by a psychiatrist, which he thought was very helpful. Despite his unhappy childhood, he was very good with his students and was well-liked by everyone. He was kind hearted, compassionate, caring, understanding, and loving towards everyone, including at home, in school, and in church.

SPIRITUAL HISTORY:

He thanked his parents for the gift of his Catholic faith, which he cherished and was able to share with others. He was a devout Catholic and active in his own parish.

CLINICAL DIAGNOSIS:

This is the case of a 60-year-old married gentleman who has disturbing OCD signs and symptoms that became noticeable when he was a teenager. He grew up in an abusive home and as the oldest child in a family of five; his father had many expectations of him. It was hard to please his father and he was always in trouble. Whenever he did not do things to paternal specifications, he was severely criticized. When he made any mistakes, he was punished harshly. His father is very old now, but remains very mean to everyone, especially to him. As a result, he turned to alcohol growing up, a bad habit only worsened in the military. He got married and initially had a rough adjustment because his wife was also demanding. In time, with marital therapy, they learned to adjust to each other and have a good understanding of one another. He also had fears of losing his wife to illness, but his wife is relatively healthy.

His Stress Audit revealed high family, personal, environmental, and work stressors. He showed elevated symptomatology in the muscular, vascular, cognitive, and emotional areas. He denied any depression but he showed high level of anxiety. His Mental Status Exam revealed someone who was age appropriate in his appearance, but overweight. He was dressed neatly and he was well groomed. He was cooperative, responsive to every question, and his responses were appropriate. Speech was normal in tone and speed. His mood was anxious and he denied any suicidal thoughts. He never experienced delusions or hallucinations. His sensorium and cognitive functioning were intact. His thought content revolved around his OCD symptoms, which included the following:

- Needing to check and re-check things
- Needing to walk in a particular pattern
- Frequently counting as he did things

- Frequently hand washing to the point that his hands were rough and raw
- Many repetitive and time consuming rituals he felt compelled to do
- Uncontrollable fears that would set in when he did not do what he was thinking
- Tremendous anxiety before and during the performing of his rituals
- His work had to be done to perfection
- Plenty of energy to repeat the work at hand
- Persistent impulses to do things a certain way
- Extremely demanding and orderly in his yard work, just as when he was a child
- Meticulous in his work and environment
- Poor listening skills when he pre-occupied with obsessive thoughts
- Excessive cleaning
- Ruminating over things
- Scrupulosity, often with worries about sinning
- Preoccupation with sequencing things

He was very receptive in dealing with his unresolved issues with his father. He was able to write him a letter and felt good about what he said. He forgave his father. He started to affirm himself and challenged his negative self-talk. He was trained in relaxation exercises with biofeedback to learn to control his responses and learn self-regulation. He continued to take his medications.

Case B

This is the case of a 39-year-old widow who complained of music running in her head and hearing continuous persecutory voices telling her to commit suicide. The voices were so relentless that she could not focus, was unable to drive, and had to stop working.

PRESENTING PROBLEMS:

She was dating a man who participated in black magic. They were sexually involved and lived together for a few years. Even though she was a Catholic, she was not practicing her Faith. She allowed this man to get her into occult activities as well as the New Age movement. The relationship abruptly ended when her boyfriend died. She eventually married a man twice her age, but he died suddenly from a heart attack. She found out that her husband had been unfaithful and had a number of mistresses in his life. While visiting her husband's gravesite, she felt a surge of energy enter her body and experienced horrible visual images. Since that time, she had heard these voices in her head that repeatedly told her how bad she was. The horrific music went on and on. She felt sexually stimulated by some forces that led to sexual orgasm.

MEDICAL HISTORY:

She was a healthy adult with no previous medical or surgical history.

FAMILY HISTORY:

She was the only child of a tumultuous marriage. Her parents eventually divorced, but it was a bitter separation. Her mother was unfaithful, had affairs with married men, and was self-centered. Her father was nasty and tape-recorded every interaction. There was much tension. She was only 6 years old when the parents divorced and she never saw her father again.

EDUCATIONAL HISTORY:

She went to public schools but did not finish high school. She dropped out to spend time with friends.

PSYCHOLOGICAL HISTORY:

She was desperate for help with her condition. She went to see a psychiatrist since she felt like she was losing her mind. She was put on anti-psychotic and anti-anxiety medications. After taking the medications for a year, the symptoms persisted, so she was referred for psychotherapy. She had been depressed since she was a child secondary to the lonely home environment in which she grew up. She attempted suicide as a teenager by overdosing and she ran away from home on a number of occasions.

SPIRITUAL HISTORY:

She was baptized a Catholic, but did not live in a Catholic home. As a child, she grew up witnessing the fighting of her parents. She did not have any Catholic formation. She came complaining of the following diabolical attacks:

- Tormented by unrelenting, uncontrollable evil thoughts
- The voices in her head wanted her dead
- She was physically shaken and held down by some unforeseen forces
- There was an evil presence near her and she saw dark, evil images in her room
- She heard eerie and unexplainable noises
- Something would shake her bed, turn on her computer, and turn up the volume of her radio
- She felt a heavy feeling of evil presence in her
- Objects would fly and move inexplicably
- She felt under attack in her finances, her health, and her relationships
- She felt blocked in the things she wants to do
- She had physical discomforts that could not be medically explained

As she looked back into her past life, she realized that she opened the door to the evil one by her poor choices. She made herself vulnerable by:

- Playing with a Ouija board when she was a teenager
- Playing with tarot cards
- Consulting a psychic on numerous occasions
- Addicted to visiting a palm reader since she was anxious about her future
- Reading astrology and horoscopes
- Collecting crystals that she was told has powers
- Listening to heavy metal music and hanging out with gothic youths

CLINICAL DIAGNOSIS:

This is the case of a 39-year-old widow who came with a friend. The patient appeared sad, defeated, helpless, and hopeless about her condition. She was prescribed a variety of anti-psychotic medications, but nothing was working.

She was extremely discouraged, overwhelmed, and anxious if she would ever get any relief. She could not sleep at night as she went to bed with fear, for the assaults and even worsened at night. She lost weight since she had poor appetite and coped with her nervousness by chain smoking. She has a limited support system since she was estranged from her family of origin. She was very fearful and lacked confidence in herself.

Her Stress Audit showed very high family, personal, social, environmental, and financial stressors. She showed elevated symptoms in the following areas: muscular, cardiovascular, emotional, cognitive, endocrine, and immune systems. Her vulnerability to stress was also high with a poor support system and poor health habits. She showed moderately high anxiety and depressive signs and symptoms. Her personality showed a sanguine-phlegmatic temperament. Her mental status exam showed a well groomed, well dressed, underweight woman who looked frail. She complained of feeling out of control but her behavior was gentle, cooperative, and she appeared a reliable source of information. She needed much assurance. Her speech was soft and slow and its content was focused on the evil attacks happening to her. She appeared anxious and her perceptions could have been interpreted as someone having visual, tactile, and auditory hallucinations. However, even a friend of hers had noticed unusual things that had gone on in that house and was afraid to admit actually having seen dark images briefly run through the walls.

She was oriented to time, place, and person. She had good recent memory but some struggles with her past memories, many of which were painful to recall. Her immediate recall was good and she was able to focus on math computations. Her general knowledge, ability to abstract, and judgment were intact. She was badly in need of help and willing to cooperate with whatever might help her. She returned to the sacraments and began going to weekly Mass. She started wearing sacramentals and had a priest bless her house. She was referred to priests in the diocese to pray over her. She was compliant with all the recommendations of the priests and a lay person who prayed over her. She finally found some relief and was able to live without the constant harassment of evil forces. Her medications were discontinued by her psychiatrist.

CHAPTER 8

IS THIS DIABOLICAL INFESTATION OR HALLUCINATION?

Case A

A 49-year-old Christian man was brought in by his wife. He complained that he was being tortured by the evil one so he felt helpless and victimized. The wife was concerned though she was not in full agreement with his perception of the problems. She related that every day her husband remarked to her that he heard mean, sadistic, threatening words inside his head that made him feel he was going crazy.

PRESENTING PROBLEMS:

Around the year 2000, he picked up a book that was about the Old Testament and numerology. He became very involved and extremely preoccupied with this topic. He was so involved that he started feeling peculiar things: the sensation that somebody was tapping on his skin, chronic headaches, and insomnia. He said, "I've been fighting with the demons. I am tortured by horrible thoughts. They speak to me all day long with many voices in my head. I feel like my head is packed with demons." He heard voices and sounds and saw ghost-like images in his room. The worst attacks occurred at night, which made it hard for him to get any rest. Consequently, he had not been able to work for years. He was relying on his wife to support the family. He had isolated himself and was afraid of the demons transferring to someone else. He felt attacked in his environment. He felt his own cat was behaving differently because it was scratching him often. He saw images of spirit-like creatures around the house. The wife did not understand what was going on with her husband and she did not recognize this man because this was not the same person she married 25 years ago. She was raised a pagan, but had become Christian Scientist. Her husband complained to her of spirits going into the cat litter. He smelled cat feces and urine everywhere in the house, which was a disgusting, awful smell. The wife did not see any physical evidence of these changes, but her husband was very convinced and he constantly fought with her on this issue.

MEDICAL HISTORY:

He had a normal childhood. He was healthy and enjoyed spending time outdoors. He was strong and physically active and involved doing manual work. As an adult, he developed diabetes mellitus, headaches, hypertension, and a sleep disorder. He actually saw his physician and was given medications for his high blood pressure. He refused to take any other medications and was non-compliant. He had not seen his primary care provider for the past five years. He had been refusing to go anywhere until his wife convinced him to come to the office. He took vitamins and fish oil. He was a non-smoker, denied illicit drug use, and the last alcohol drink was 25 years ago.

FAMILY HISTORY:

He was the youngest son in a family of three boys. His father still lived with him and supported him. His dad shared the story of his very active, athletic son who helped him in their landscaping business in his younger years. His mother passed away 15 years ago. As the father got older, he decided to have his dad live with him so they could look out for each other. He was married, but he and his wife did not have any biological children together. His wife was previously married and had two children from that marriage.

EDUCATIONAL HISTORY:

He went to public school and did not pursue college since he was very involved in the family business. He wanted to earn a living at an early age and enjoyed working side by side with his father. He learned to play the guitar and had a great love for music. He composed songs and he loved to sing.

PSYCHOLOGICAL HISTORY:

Since they always lived on the farm, they did not know much about illness. Everybody had some type of home remedy for every malady. The father could not give any meaningful psychiatric history on either side of the family. The most common response to any weird behavior was not to talk about it and to deny it existed. In this case, it could not be ignored because it affected the lives of those living with him. Despite his repeated refusal, he finally agreed to see a psychiatrist. He was prescribed an anti-psychotic medication which he took because it helped put him to sleep. His wife observed that he was actually better and was doing well. The problem was his refusal to get a refill when he ran out of the medicine. He said he was feeling fine and he did not need any medication. His wife described him as a caring, good hearted, and honest man. However, in the past eight years he had become cruel, uncaring, self-centered, and erratic in his behavior. Due to his irrational behavior, his wife had him committed against his will and so he was hospitalized for a few days. He was better after taking what was prescribed at the hospital, but he eventually stopped it again.

SPIRITUAL HISTORY:

He was born and raised as a Christian. As a Southern Baptist, he loved the Bible as a young man. He said his prayers regularly and went to church every Sunday. Since he got worse eight years ago, he had not gone back to church. He denied any involvement with the occult or any such activities. He listed the following diabolical attacks, but his wife had not observed any of these:

- Being tormented by unrelenting and uncontrollable evil thoughts
- Evil forces surrounding him and attacking him
- Being physically shaken and held down by unforeseen forces
- Hearing knocking on the walls
- Seeing the evil presence of dark images walking in his room or sitting at the edge of the bed
- Hearing eerie, inexplicable noises, such as voices of women in the house

- Hearing screaming, vile, profane, blasphemous language the time he burned a Bible
- Feeling his bedroom was haunted with peculiar smell and sounds

CLINICAL DIAGNOSIS:

This is the case of a 49-year-old married man who was accompanied by his wife. He had a facial expression of someone who was not in touch with reality. He complained of demonic attacks, but he presented his ideas like someone with auditory, visual, and tactile hallucinations. He even described his eyes as being scratched and with planks being left in his eyes. He complained of having hair in his throat and no matter how hard he tried, he could not get rid of it. He also remarked that something was stimulating him and having sex with him. He complained of itchiness and burning sensations in his legs. His wife would not agree to these bizarre descriptions: in her view, these were the ravings of a lunatic, and her husband had been sane previously. She remarked that her husband has completely changed and she had seen him go downhill in the past eight years due to his refusal to take his anti-psychotic medications regularly. When he was taking his medicines, he was able to function normally, did house work and yard work. She could not convince him to resume taking his medications.

He appeared much older than his age. He was tall and well-built. His hair was disheveled and his clothes were casual and wrinkled. He often seemed overwhelmed by his thoughts, which he could not express in a coherent manner. Concentration was difficult and he was not a reliable informant. He was suspicious, hyper-vigilant, argumentative, restless and agitated. Speech was rapid and pressured a reflection of his anxiety. His affect was incongruous with his speech. He denied any suicidal thoughts or any previous suicide attempts. He had perceptual distortions and somatic delusions. He was oriented to person and place but not to time. While his general knowledge was intact, he had impaired judgment and difficulty with mathematical calculations. He was ambivalent about getting help and considered his condition as purely spiritual, not psychological. As I summarized his entire problem, he realized he needed help and was willing to be seen in therapy. He finally agreed to see a physician and take medication to help him sleep. His doctor prescribed quetiapine, which helped his sleep as well as his distorted thinking. In later visits, he appeared calmer, his mind was clearer, his level of suspicion diminished, and he became confident he could resume driving. He invited a Catholic priest to bless his house and he felt much better since he was no longer bothered by troubling images, pestering sounds, or disgusting smells.

Case B

A 55-year-old divorced man complained of strange things happening in his house. He felt that there were evil spirits attacking him after he attended a charismatic movement event. He was scared about weird things happening to his pets. Even his daughter was seeing dark images and heard banging of objects against the wall.

PRESENTING PROBLEMS:

Two years ago, he went to a charismatic movement event and ever since then, unusual things were happening to him and his environment. He went into a meditative state and felt a vibration in his hypogastric area. He heard banging sounds and items fell inside the shower every morning at 3:00 A.M. He did not see anyone causing the problems. The nightly occurrences made it hard for him to sleep. He also felt that there was a spirit attacking him. Even his dogs were acting weird and looking at something he could not see. Nevertheless, the dogs were scared and kept moving as if avoiding something in the house.

MEDICAL HISTORY:

Since he was a child, he had suffered from headaches but he just accepted it as part of his life. The only medications he was prescribed was for allergies. He used to smoke marijuana when he was a teenager. He suffered from aches and pains in his body, especially in his joints.

FAMILY HISTORY:

He described his childhood as horrible. He came from a Catholic family with eight children. He felt gaps in his memory due to physical, sexual, and emotional abuses of the past. He was very young when his mother died. He recalled living with different people after his mother's death, including neighbors, his grandmother, then finally his father after he remarried. Sadly, his stepmother was abusive and suffered from mental illness. He had to live with the vacillating emotions of his stepmother, who was physically cruel towards him since he was the most outspoken and often defended his siblings. He was sexually abused in his younger years, including a sexual assault by his stepbrother when he was older.

The biological mother's side of the family had problems with alcoholism, homosexuality, and law-breaking behavior. He described his mother's side as having much "darkness," the details about which he was unclear, but there were definitely lots of emotional and legal problems.

In later years, his siblings became alcoholics and one of his brothers committed suicide.

EDUCATIONAL HISTORY:

He graduated from college with a few credits towards a masters' degree. He served in the military.

PSYCHOLOGICAL HISTORY

In college, he was introduced to alcohol and smoking marijuana, both of which he abused for a few years. These in turn led to other immoral activities. He occasionally struggled with depression, but he did not seek help. He abused alcohol when he was in the military because he was a victim of sodomy. He reacted to this trauma by living a promiscuous life. He became very depressed.

He had suicidal attempts when he was going through a rough time with the suicide of his own brother. He was previously seen for counseling by a therapist when he was out of the country for a military assignment and again in another state for a different assignment. He was wondering if he was having visual, auditory, and tactile hallucinations with the things going on in his life.

SPIRITUAL HISTORY:

He was raised as a Catholic and was married in the Church. Despite the bad things that happened in his life, he remained fervent in his prayers. Since his mother died when he was young, he did not recall that they ever prayed as a family. What he remembered were disruptions in their lives since he and his siblings had an unstable home situation with multiple moves. His family of origin lived in a house that was scary for the children since they were seeing ghosts. His siblings played with Ouija board, so he was exposed to it. He became involved with the New Age movement when he was traveling as an adult and was not going to church for a period of time.

In one of the houses where he previously lived, a man had died there and he sensed something spooky about the house. He was told that bad things happened there. He found himself seeking palm reading, fortune telling, and trying to connect with the dead. Since he returned to the Catholic Church, he realized the bad choices he had made and how they impacted his present life.

CLINICAL DIAGNOSIS:

This is the case of a 55-year-old divorced man who complained of unusual things happening in his house, which prevented him from sleeping. Night after night, there were disturbances in his shower and even the dogs were howling because they were seeing something. At all hours of the day and night, the dogs acted like they were avoiding something. Even his own daughter remarked she had heard the banging on the walls, but she could not see anyone. Headaches and body aches remained a persistent problem.

He was highly anxious with restlessness, irritability, apprehension, excessive sweating, frequent urination, tension and fear of the dark. He was feeling depressed, lacking sleep, experiencing nightmares and fatigue. At work, he was getting easily distracted, lacking focus, and becoming forgetful. His boss had warned him about his poor performance and inability to get the work done in a timely manner.

His physical appearance was that of an overweight adult gentleman who appeared age appropriate. He was dressed casually and neatly. At the time of the interview, he appeared to be generally in control. He was cooperative and willingly provided information. His speech was rapid and pressured. His speech content was focused on the weird events in his house. He needed reassurance wondering if he was losing his mind because of his bizarre complaints. He was anxious and somewhat restless. He complained about difficulty focusing, periods of confusion, racing thoughts, and getting easily distracted. His sensorium and cognitive functioning were intact. He realized his need for professional help since his job was getting compromised.

His Stress Audit showed acute and chronic stress with very high scores. His high stressors were coming from family, personal, social, environmental, financial, and work related issues. His stress manifestations were highly elevated in the muscular, gastro-intestinal, cardiac, emotional, cognitive, endocrine, and immune systems.

He had a strong personality and he was outspoken. He was choleric and melancholic in his temperament. He did not care about what other people think and he did what he thought was right. Because of his exacting standards, he was hard to satisfy. He was driven and exhausted all possibilities before he came to any conclusion. He focused on gathering data, which complemented his job with computers. He was highly competitive and sets a high standard for his performance. Because he had to weigh everything so carefully, he had some difficulty with making decisions, which led to delays in resolution of the issue and sometimes resulted in his inability to make a final decision. He had a tendency to work late and was considered a night owl to the point of having difficulty falling asleep.

As we proceeded with therapy, it became more and more clear that he was suffering from a bipolar disorder.

- Racing thoughts that led to rapid, pressured speech.
- Periods of having so much energy that he could literally stay up all night.
- Difficulties with anger, impatience, being verbally abusive, and easily prone to rage
- Sexually hyperactive and abusing pornography
- Everybody who knew him complained about his mood swings
- He was always seeking pleasurable activities, even to the point of taking risks
- Periods of depression for years

He was receptive and was referred to a psychiatrist for medication evaluation. He responded well to the mood stabilizer and anti-depressant medications. He felt much better, but the noises and banging at night did not stop. A priest was consulted in his parish. Two priests went to bless his home and outside the home. They prayed over him and his daughter. The dogs were quiet while the priests prayed over the place. After that time, there were no longer unusual occurrences in the house.

CHAPTER 9

IS THIS DIABOLICAL POSSESSION OR DISSOCIATIVE DISORDER?

Case A

This is the case of a 37-year-old Catholic woman who was born in Peru and married to a non-practicing Buddhist with three daughters. She was high-functioning and worked as a part-time investment broker. She was brought in by her husband, who was very concerned about her recent behavior. She admitted that she did not know what happened, but something had taken over her.

PRESENTING PROBLEMS:

She complained of a sudden change in her behavior as witnessed by her husband and other people at a party when she acted bizarrely and her eyes looked so evil that people around her got scared. She was shouting profanities and was so strong that four men had to hold her down. She was saying things that no one should know about people at the party. The information shared was private so she should have had no knowledge of it at all. She claimed she was Lucifer. The voice that came out of her said, "She is weak and I have taken her over. I am also taking over her mother and brother." When holy water was sprinkled on her, she shouted that she was burning and cursed everyone in the room. Her husband was fearful of her ever since he witnessed this incident. Her mother was called to the scene. Her mother whispered prayers in their native language into her ears. After this, something left her: she quieted down and fell asleep. Her family took her to the emergency department to be checked, but there her work-up was negative. She had no memories of the entire event, except what she was told by her husband and her friends.

Prior to this event, she had previously experienced weird situations. She felt like she was in a trance and she could actually see things that she normally should not know. She was working out at a gym when she felt compelled to approach a woman who was also working out to share with her what she saw in a trance. She saw her lying down with candles surrounding her. To the other woman's amazement, she confided that her husband has been threatening her with a knife and told her that he has plans of killing her. This alerted both of them.

When she went to visit her native country, she had two unusual incidents in which she rapidly cycled between laughing and crying. Her brothers were witnesses to these events. She recalled that her maternal grandfather died in her arms in that same time frame. When she was at the beach sitting by the water, she saw a black, evil creature that made her cry hysterically. She lost consciousness. When she regained consciousness, she could not understand what happened to her and her relatives explained to her what they witnessed. Her entire experience was bizarre.

MEDICAL HISTORY:

She was born a healthy child with normal growth and development. She had no previous surgeries and no illnesses. She had environmental allergies.

FAMILY HISTORY:

She was the youngest child of five with four brothers. For no clear reason, her father did not believe that she was his daughter. Her father was mean and abusive towards the children. She was twelve when her father was murdered. The family members commented that her father had a mysterious past. He was born in his parents' house at the same moment that their neighbor across the street, who was a witch, passed away. They all felt something happened to the baby boy at that time. Her father grew up a distant, quiet, unemotional person. He was very demanding and angry, which earned him many enemies. Sometimes his fights were so severe that he ended in prison. When he got married, he did not change. There was a feeling of darkness that followed him, to the point that her mother remarked that it seemed like there was another person in between them in bed, some type of unseen dark forces that surrounded him. After he passed away, she was raised by her mother and her maternal grandparents.

EDUCATIONAL HISTORY:

She went to public school, but they went to church regularly and she received religious education. She took college courses, but only finished two years of college.

PSYCHOLOGICAL HISTORY:

She was a teenager when she sought counseling for family issues. She revealed to her family that her maternal grandfather and her paternal uncle sexually abused her. She only went for a few sessions and did not have any further counseling for her past traumas. Her problems were never resolved and she kept things inside.

SPIRITUAL HISTORY:

She was baptized and received the sacraments of Penance and Holy Communion. She did not recall if she was confirmed. She attended weekly Mass. She moved to the United States of America and got married in the Catholic Church. She was prayed over often and even attended daily Mass.

CLINICAL DIAGNOSIS:

This is the case of a 37-year-old, married woman who was worried about the recent events in her life. She could not explain what happened to her and she was worried that her husband was afraid of her and distancing himself, which was impairing their ability to communicate. They were having marital problems. Prior to this, she had a bizarre incident at a neighborhood party. She was talking to a friend when she started sharing information that she should have not known. The friend who was listening to her was surprised and the information was validated. She had previous experiences of falling into a trance and being able to predict what was going to happen. At that party, she suddenly acted in a strange way, shouting profanities, and her body was moving so violently that she could not be held down by four men. She seemed extraordinarily strong. She normally was a kind, sweet, delightful, feminine woman who would neither act belligerently nor say any profanities. The police were called but they could not do anything. When holy water was sprinkled on her, she shouted that she was burning and cursed at the people around her, demanding that they leave. Her mother was called and immediately came to her side, whispering prayers to her ears and she became calm again. Once she quieted down and fell asleep, she was taken to the nearby emergency room where a computerized tomography (CT) scan of the head was done and medical examination was performed. They could not find a plausible explanation for her scary behavior. She had no recollection of what took place that evening, except for what was shared by the eyewitnesses. The following events comprised her manifestation:

- Something evil had completely taken over against her will
- Involuntary movements propelled by some forces
- Irrational and scary behavior
- A voice that was not hers, which had an eerie and evil tone, came out from her
- Vile, profane, blasphemous language was used
- Extreme, superhuman strength appearing supernatural
- Her eyes rolled up with an evil expression
- Revealing things that she should have not known
- An aversion to the holy water

She recovered from the incident and was taken to their local priest, who prayed over her. She went to confession and made a novena to the Holy Spirit before she scheduled another deliverance prayer. She went to a church to be prayed over by a priest and a local lay healer. She fully recovered and returned to her usual self. She frequented going to Mass and went to regular confession while wearing sacramentals. However, after that one bizarre incident at a party, that one event deeply affected her and her family. She became nervous and anxious. She complained of becoming forgetful, having poor concentration, making frequent mistakes and suffering from chronic fatigue.

Her psychological testing revealed no evidence of depression, but she had remarkable anxiety, even though her self-report was showing low scores. Her Stress Audit revealed acute and chronic stress with higher symptoms than stressors. She showed elevated muscular, cardiovascular, cognitive, and endocrine signs and symptoms. She had high vulnerability to stress as she demonstrated poor health habits and the inability to share her thoughts and feelings, despite the presence of supportive family members. She showed a melancholic-phlegmatic temperament. Her Mental Status Exam revealed an age-appropriate, well dressed, neatly attired attractive woman whose curly long hair was neatly tied into a ponytail. She appeared in control and her behavior was calm and cooperative. She needed a lot of reassurance that her diabolical attack was not going to happen again. She learned about spiritual warfare. Her speech was soft and gentle but sometimes showed apprehension. Her mood was anxious. She denied suicidal ideation and previous suicidal attempts. In interviewing her, she has past unresolved traumas that she kept inside and never talked about again. Her orientation to time, place, and person were intact. She was able recall past, recent, and immediate information. She was able to do simple mathematical calculations and her general knowledge, judgment, and abstract formation were intact. Her thought content seemed to be preoccupied with ways to rebuild her marriage after the incident that created tremendous fear on the part of her husband.

Case B

A 41-year-old single woman came with a long history of headaches. She had attempted various treatments, but to no avail. She tried biofeedback with a male therapist but she was uncomfortable working with a man. She was hoping to have the same successful result as her colleague, whom I had treated, who referred her to me so she wanted to see a female therapist which was her preference.

PRESENTING PROBLEMS:

She recounted having had headaches since she was a child. Three years ago, the headaches intensified. She described the headaches to be across the forehead, down the temples, usually with a sensation of pressure on top of the head, but at times the pain could be stabbing, throbbing, or pulsating with the beating of her heart. She had sensitivity to light and the headaches occurred daily. Distractions, such as her favorite hobby, helped to reduce the pain. However, too much sensory stimulation made her headache worse. She rated her headache as eight to nine on a scale of 0 to 10 with ten being the worst pain. She would be awakened at night by the headaches. She has missed work since the pain would render her unable to function because of its intensity and her inability to sleep. She experienced memory problems and lapses in recalling her history.

MEDICAL HISTORY:

She gave a long history of doctors she consulted for her headaches and was tried on a variety of medications, including narcotics. She did not like being on medications with the potential for being addictive, so she switched doctors to find alternative forms of treatment. She had numerous emergency room visits to alleviate excruciating headaches. The last medication that seemed to help some was nortriptyline.

FAMILY HISTORY:

She was the fourth child of a family of six. Her parents were in their 70s, but she does not have any communication with them. She had alienated herself for survival since the family had too much psychiatric pathology. Her brothers were alcoholics and other siblings also suffered from headaches.

EDUCATIONAL HISTORY:

She had a college degree specializing in her area of work.

PSYCHOLOGICAL HISTORY:

She grew up in an abusive home. She was physically, emotionally, and sexually abused by her own father. Her abuses were frequent and so severe at times that she lost consciousness after being hit repeatedly on the head. In order to deal with the abuses, she used to numb her body so as not to feel the pain or she pretended to be an observer and not the victim. She used to hide in the closet so that she could disappear, but her father always found her. She had difficulty trusting people.

She had a history of psychiatric hospitalizations and saw a number of therapists through the years. She suffered from depression and anxiety, but her more serious diagnosis was dissociative identity disorder (multiple personality). She remarked that she had as many as eight different personalities. Her roommates, who were concerned about her mental health and concerned about not knowing with whom they were dealing, often told her about these personalities. She was generally quiet and passive so roommates really liked her.

SPIRITUAL HISTORY:

She was a baptized Catholic but had not been attending any church since she thought her parents were hypocrites. They were going to church and telling children to go, but the parents behavior was so contrary to the Christian teachings that they learned. She eventually returned to church as an adult and found a church in which she felt comfortable. She believed in God and knew that God loves her. She developed good friendships in the church. She received support from her pastor and her church community.

CLINICAL DIAGNOSIS:

This is the case of a 41-year-old single woman with a presenting problem of headaches but had a more serious problem with dissociative disorder. She came with downcast facies and her speech was slow, soft and gentle. She was slim and appropriately attired. She looked insecure and her posture was bent forward. She had learned relaxation exercises before and wanted to be trained on biofeedback to help control her headaches. She complained of a sleep disorder due to her headaches. She also had muscle tension, forgetfulness, poor concentration, difficulty expressing herself, anxiety, restlessness, and irritability. She also had anger and frustration.

Her Headache Questionnaire revealed a combination of muscular and vascular headaches. Her frequent use of computers aggravated her headaches. Her headache was daily and at times could be crippling to the point of being unable to function, forcing her to stay in bed under the covers.

Her Stress Audit revealed high personal, social, and work stressors. Her stress manifestations were high in the muscular, vascular, gastro-intestinal, cognitive and emotional areas. She demonstrated acute and chronic stress.

Her anxiety rating was high, but her depression was equally elevated. She contracted for safety, reassuring me that she was not going to harm herself. She was overwhelmed with all the demands at work. She got discouraged when she was told that her work was not good enough.

She was receptive to the recommendations I made regarding lifestyle adjustments. Her headaches started to improve when she changed her daily routine. After successfully identifying food triggers for her migraines, she was able to avoid them. She continued to practice her relaxation exercises. She paced herself and did not allow the pressures of work to get to her. She listened to relaxation and affirmation tapes at bedtime. As a result, she was sleeping better and was waking up rested.

During this time, her mother contacted her regarding the death of a relative. She was upset that her mother called her because she hated that her mother was an alcoholic and did not protect her from all the abuses when she was a child. She had not forgiven her parents for what happened to her. Her headaches the following week increased. That week, her two trusted doctors were going out of the country on a vacation. She expressed concern that they were not going to be available. I assured her that I would be staying in town and available to her if she needed me. While she was in therapy relaxing, she suddenly opened her eyes, stared blankly for a period of time, then asked me with a puzzled look who I was and what was she doing there. I calmed her down and introduced myself. I further explained where she was and what we were trying to accomplish. I asked her who she thought she was. She gave me a different name and this person was more assertive, questioning everything we were doing. With the help of her friend, who had been in the waiting room, she was assured to be in a safe place and that I was there to help her. She calmed down and as she relaxed, she eventually returned to her main personality. She was upset and apologetic that she switched personalities, but we discussed the current situation in her life and how that could have contributed to the stress, which made her feel threatened. She understood and felt better. As the therapy progressed, her headaches were under control. However, she was not quite ready to deal with her multiple personalities and attempt to integrate them. She was happy not to suffer from daily headaches and to be sleeping restfully at night.

RECOMMENDATIONS
FOR TREATMENT

"Pray with great confidence, with confidence based upon the goodness and infinite generosity of God and upon the promises of Jesus Christ. God is a spring of living water which flows unceasingly into the hearts of those who pray."

—St. Louis de Montfort

CHAPTER 10

RECOMMENDATIONS FOR TREATMENT

The clinical diagnosis is the determining factor in the treatment plan of care. Make sure that the patient receives feedback on the results of all medical records and testing so that, together with the patient, plans for treatment may be formulated. A multi-faceted approach is usually the most effective form of treatment. The following protocol is my usual method for treating various psychiatric conditions. My approach to healing involves non-pharmacological approaches, which constitutes my recommended treatment plan. If the patient requires medication as part of the treatment protocol, this recommendation must be made to the primary care physician or psychiatrist. Their recommendations will be discussed with the patient to ensure that there is good understanding regarding the importance of taking medication as prescribed by a physician. Otherwise, here are the areas that need to be addressed with the patient.

I. Ensure that the activities of daily living are stable and well established.
A. Sleep Pattern
B. Eating Habits
C. Exercise Program
II. Challenge irrational or distorted belief systems.
III. Control presenting signs and symptoms
IV. Increase mobility and daily functioning

V.   Allow freedom of expression about disturbing thoughts and feelings

VI.   Monitor and increase accountability of the patient regarding managing one's problems

VII.   Avoid any communication problem with spouse or family members by including them in the treatment and discussion.

VIII.   Address unresolved issues of childhood that may be a stumbling block to healing.

IX.   Address any unresolved traumas of the past.

X.   Address the need for self-forgiveness and the need to forgive people who may have offended the patient

Some patients may have multiple co-morbidities so it is important to address the concurrent problems. There is a high percentage of personality disorder occurring with the primary condition, thus making the treatment more complicated. Many patients may benefit from family therapy or couples therapy. Referral to support groups in order to address addictions, such as Alcoholics Anonymous (AA), Narcotics Anonymous (NA), Sexaholics Anonymous (SA), just to name a few, will be beneficial for long term recovery. The patient may be referred to group therapy or to area agencies, which may help resolve these other issues.

Diabolical conditions need extra approaches. I usually complete all the needed assessment and evaluation, then a comprehensive report must be given to the referring priest. If the case is more serious, such as a diabolical possession, then a written report to the local bishop or the requesting bishop is required in order to request for exorcism. As previously mentioned in the book, it is important that a psychiatrist be involved at this level to ensure that all psychiatric conditions have been ruled out. In many cases, attempts must be made to assist the patient through the help of local priests or lay people gifted in dealing with spiritual warfare. In this way, if the problem resolves, then immediate help is given to the patient. Getting hold of an exorcist is not an easy matter. There is a shortage of exorcists in the United States, even throughout the world. If an exorcism were to be recommended, it is mandated that an Exorcism Release Form (Exhibit F) be signed to protect the entire team involved in the process. This is a serious matter requiring that the patient and/or designated guardian and/or authorized representative be made aware of what will be done and their consent is critical to this process.

Here are some recommended approaches to patients with a diabolical condition:

- Approach the patient calmly and prayerfully. Be aware that retaliation is to be expected from the other side. Be on your guard, armed with your faith. Fast and pray for this case.
- Direct the patient to sit down even though the patient may end up on the floor as the manifestations occur.
- Ensure the safety of the patient by putting the patient in a room that has enough space. I have a room with padded flooring and padded furniture with no objects around that could hurt the patient.
- Recommend for another person to contact a priest who might be available to pray over the patient, if not, simply ask them to pray. This individual could be your secretary or another therapist. I usually have a prayer group, especially my friends in the Legion of Mary (a Catholic lay organization) whom I can depend on to pray whenever I request. You may request for prayers from the religious sisters or religious brothers or any other religious group with whom you may be connected or have had previous contact.
- Sprinkle the room immediately with holy water and holy salt. Ahead of time, I request a priest to pray over and bless boxes of salt and bottles of water using exorcism prayers.
- Have a crucifix and special prayers available for such cases. These prayers are available at the end of the book. Keep praying until the manifestation slows down. The patient is not free from the evil one; the manifestations are simply not overt.
- Patients are usually upset as to why they have no control over the evil one. They are embarrassed about what happened or they may not realize what happened and find themselves on the floor, not knowing how they got there.
- Provide support and caring. Pray with the patients to alleviate their anxiety and fear.
- Assure them of the unconditional love of God as the Heavenly Father who has power and wisdom that supersedes any of His creatures.

- Since there are usually concurrent psychological conditions, address whatever the presenting problem is, just like a regular psychiatric patient.
- Offer hope and refer the patient to a clergy/priest and a clinician who may be able to help the patient if you are uncomfortable and feel unable to help this patient. The involvement of a priest is critical in dealing with this diabolical condition and in returning the person to the Faith and to the sacraments. Direct the patients to help themselves by returning to the healing sacrament of confession (Penance) and the frequent reception of the sacraments, especially the Holy Communion (Holy Eucharist). They can benefit from wearing sacramentals and having other forms of sacramentals in the house.
- Ensure availability of support from the family members, such as the spouse or the parents. At times, the closest person could be a friend or a neighbor who can keep an eye on the person. The family members themselves could use support since they are dealing with a condition that is not only unfamiliar to them, but also scary.
- Request for house and car blessings from the clergy for the safe return of the patient to them.
- Conferring with the psychiatrist who is also caring for the patient is helpful for the adjustment of medication since the diabolical manifestation is traumatic to every patient, considered as a violation of self or an attack on them. If there is no current psychiatrist, referral to one is good for initial evaluation and potential medication. Many patients prefer referral to their primary care physician with whom they have had previous contact and a long-term relationship.
- It is possible that patients may not be receptive to medications. Explain the reason for the prescription and the final decision will be with the physician.
- If referral for further psychological testing is necessary, then do so. These test results can help confirm the observations of the clinician.
- Do not allow the patient to leave until stable and a support system is available to them. At times, the patient may stay in the office for hours. Time is not the issue. Safety of the patient is the real issue.
- Privacy of the patient must be ensured. Make sure that other patients are not affected or scandalized. I prefer to see the patient in the back room away from the other patients so the flow of the office is not directly

affected, even though it may affect other clinicians' appointments with other patients. Treat this condition as if one suddenly has a psychotic patient in the office. These are unpredictable cases, but they have to be managed discreetly.

- Encourage the patient to have a daily, consistent prayer life. Provide assistance if they are unfamiliar or again refer to a priest.
- Guide the patients to read spiritually uplifting religious books that can help with the situation.
- If an exorcism is required, make sure the patient and significant other (family member) sign the release to be able offer this service. In our practice, we have a particular liability release form to protect us when we are trying to help a patient. In general, it is imperative for the patient to sign this form to be able to talk or give information to a priest or to the bishop or his designee.
- In preparation for exorcism, refer the patient to see the bishop's designated representative for such diabolical conditions. This step will help in having another priest who is really familiar with such cases assess the situation.
- Document in detail what was observed with the patient. Provide a comprehensive written report to the bishop's designee or directly to the requesting Bishop to help with the referral to an exorcist.

For the benefit of those who are not familiar with the rite of exorcism, which can only be done by a priest with the approval of the local bishop, I recommend that you ask a trusted clergy who is in good standing with the Church for a good book to read. There are specific prayers also to exorcise salt and water.

Whenever lay people are involved in the deliverance prayer over a patient, I suggest that a Catholic priest be involved since the Holy Eucharist is important to be present in praying over the patient and there is no replacement for the power of the priesthood. The patient and the lay people involved are best prepared by receiving Holy Communion on the day of prayer. It is highly recommended that fasting is done before dealing with a diabolical case since our Lord Jesus Christ Himself stated that certain cases can be best dealt with fasting and prayer (Matthew 17:20).

"Every Patient's Bill of Rights should include a statement that the patient has the right to practice his or her spirituality and religion in a respectful and supportive clinical environment. On the other hand, even the most skeptical clinician can be creatively concerned with the power of spirituality and religion rather than with their truth. Spirituality should not be disrespected in any clinical encounters. On the other hand, healthcare professionals with religious beliefs should not force religion on patients, but they should respond to the religious patient seeking some acknowledgment of his or her spirituality and religiousness and not have to worry about losing licensure for allowing a moment of silence or prayer."(S. Post, 1998, p. 21)

DISCERNMENT OF CASES: THE VALUE OF A STRONG RELIGIOUS FOUNDATION AND CLINICAL KNOWLEDGE

"This my goodness does to endow the souls of the just more fully with spiritual riches when for my love they are stripped of material goods because they have renounced the world and all its pleasures and even their own will. These are the ones who fatten their souls, enlarging them in the abyss of my charity. Then I become their spiritual provider. The Holy Spirit becomes their servant."

—St. Catherine of Siena

CHAPTER 11

DISCERNMENT OF CASES: THE VALUE OF STRONG RELIGIOUS FOUNDATION AND CLINICAL KNOWLEDGE

"I am suffering for Christ. Since I was a child, I have had all kinds of ailments, but I remained cheerful. Now, I feel attacked by the evil one. My cross is heavy."

This 40-year old, married female came with such sad facies, eyes lowered, hair disheveled, feeling helpless and frustrated with her medical providers, accusing them of not listening to her. She was a victim of emotional and physical abuse by her biological father, who was quick to get angry and violent. She was not sure if there was any family history of psychiatric condition. However, she was convinced that her father was mentally ill. He had periods of depression when he isolated himself and did not talk to anyone. On other occasions, he was enraged, accompanied by not sleeping at night. She felt rejected as a child since her father disowned her by telling her that she was an illegitimate child. She was falsely accused in school of stealing so the other students turned away from her. She also confessed to have been a victim of rape twice when she was a teenager.

In addition to emotional pain, she also suffered from physical pain. She remarked of pain all over her body, diagnosed as fibromyalgia. She staggered as she walked pausing momentarily to catch her breath since the pain was intense. Palpation of her back revealed numerous trigger points in bilateral upper trapezius muscles, rhomboid, and longissimus dorsi. She also had bilateral flank pain associated with her kidney problem. She had to reposition herself multiple times to be comfortable in her seat. She remarked that doctors were upset with her since she often came across as a drug seeker, alerting physicians to be cautious in prescribing any analgesic to her.

The history she gave included long-standing, floating anxiety, being sick all her life, and multiple previous surgeries with post-surgical complications. She claimed that she had a miracle since she almost died and somehow miraculously recovered. She has had spending problems, accumulating so much "stuff," upsetting her husband, who complained of the clutter in the house. In subsequent visits, her facial expression was that of an angry, deceitful person with rapid, pressured speech that she described as anxiety. She could go on and on talking about the various stressors in her life and how miserable she felt. At other times, she came dressed colorfully, with bright flowers in her hair, and spoke rapidly with glaring eyes.

Her medication list included anti-anxiety, anti-depressant, anti-asthma, anti-diabetes mellitus, anti-nausea, anti-diarrhea, narcotic and another medication for pain control. Her source of relief was her strong prayer life and support from God. She sought counseling and stated that her previous therapist had introduced her to the New Age Movement and beliefs, like the reincarnation, which was upsetting to her since it is so contrary to her Catholic belief. Since then, she felt under attack by the evil one and her suffering even intensified. As an adult, her life continued to be surrounded by suffering. She was not sure whether she should pray for healing or simply offer up her sufferings to God.

Her Stress Audit showed a woman who did not only have chronic stress, but acute stress. Her scores were highly elevated (99 percentile) in sources of stress, stress symptomatology, and vulnerability to stress. She denied suicidal or homicidal ideation due to her religious beliefs. Her Beck's Depression, Hamilton Anxiety Scale, and Symptom Checklist were elevated. She also remarked of not sleeping at night since her mind would not shut off, which caused an on-going marital problem. Her husband came a number of times to the session to complain of his spouse's mood swings, talking too much, excessive spending, not sleeping at night, and inability to do simple housework in the daytime. After working all day, he had to do the cooking, cleaning, and paying of the bills. He expressed frustration with his wife who was undependable and often in bed due to her pain. His wife remarked, in turn, about his excessive drinking of alcohol, addiction to pornography, lack of intimacy, and his non-communication. He often accused her of faking her symptoms and screaming at her that she was simply lazy. Their house was often a mess.

After reviewing all her symptoms, history, comments of her previous doctors, interview with her spouse, clinical observations in every session, and results of questionnaires, I had to address the need to be seen by a psychiatrist in order to be properly evaluated for her diagnosis of bipolar and the need to be prescribed appropriate medication. She was quick to identify that her father was the one who was bipolar, but she was not. She was upset with my statement and was quick to defend herself by noting that she was under spiritual attack because she was trying to be holy and obedient to the will of God. She was told by a priest that she was "a suffering soul with mystical experiences," which she was hanging on to as words of comfort to her. She refused my advice and decided not to return for more visits.

The above cited case is an illustration of one of the most common complaints I receive from patients. They are already convinced that they are under spiritual attack and refuse to consider biochemical and psychiatric conditions as a reason for their symptoms. It can not be totally ruled out that she could have diabolical oppression in addition to a psychiatric condition. The latter needs to be addressed to see to what extent the symptoms might improve with appropriate psychotherapeutic medications. However, when it is simply diabolical in nature, the other question is also raised by relatives, "How can you be sure?" or, "What made you think it is demonic?"

The same question is raised by my colleagues. The most frequent question I receive from other clinicians is, "How do you know for certain this is a diabolical case?" The response I give them is that I have ruled out other physical and psychological conditions, leaving behind only the strong evidence of a diabolical condition. I understand how perplexing it can be to deal with something that is solely spiritual, that is, without an accompanying physical and psychological explanation.

How did my practice end up seeing diabolical conditions? In 1989, I was completing my PhD when I realized I wanted to serve my clients totally in private practice. Prior to that time, I was working full-time at the hospital as Director of Education while having a small part-time clinical practice with a group of doctors. Those who have chosen private practice understand the various fears—from the loss of salary to the unchartered territory of self-sufficiency, or shall we say self-insufficiency, of running my own practice. I had to offer myself in the service of God, not knowing how I would survive. I would be armed only with faith that God is my Boss and my Provider. With the support of my husband, my ministry began and the S.T.R.E.S.S. Centre Inc. was born.

In the early 1990, I had the opportunity to meet a newly ordained priest, who became my spiritual director. My referrals increased as if God knew it was time to give me more complicated work because I had the spiritual backup. I started seeing very unusual patients whom I could not easily categorize in any particular psychiatric condition alone. I was not clinically prepared for these cases. It was not enough that I had to face these challenging cases in the daytime, but I also had to fight enemies I could not see at night. As if there were forces out there unhappy with my work, I started getting attacks of dark forces pinning me down when I was alone. I immediately went into prayer asking the Precious Blood of Jesus to cover me and summoning St. Michael the Archangel, the Holy Angels, and the Blessed Mother. After I immediately made the sign of the cross with my toes, suddenly the attacks stopped. These incidents happened a number of times, which led me to consult my spiritual director in tears and in fear. I was supported and directed on how to put on the armor of God. With blind faith, I followed his directions and I felt much relief. The spiritual cases did not stop. I received more referrals and I had to deal with them on a case by case basis. Reading a number of books on the subject matter and conferring with priests who are gifted in dealing with such cases helped me have a better grasp of the demons with which I was grappling. I was also blessed with religious sisters who I could call anytime to pray for my intentions and gifted Catholic lay healer friends, who were willing to be available to assist the priest to pray over these patients.

When I first started seeing these types of referral, I questioned God. "Why me? Why do I have to deal with such scary conditions that no instructor ever prepared me?" The response I got was, 'Why not?" In order to prepare myself to see such unique conditions, I decided to intensify my prayer life by going to daily Mass and attending silent retreats. All these helped me to listen to the whispers of God that one can only discern in quiet prayer. I knew I could not handle these patients without the help of God. He became my private instructor. I started saying spiritual warfare prayers, frequented the sacrament of confession, made the yearly St. Louis Marie the Montfort Consecration to Jesus through Mary, tried hard to stay in the state of grace, and formed a circle of prayer warriors to help me in times of serious spiritual cases. I also have my Legion of Mary friends who are more a family to me since we see each other weekly and who have been my prayer support. My own secretaries and my children became my immediate source of comfort and strength when no one else was available to help me or pray with me.

Twelve years of Catholic education helped prepare me in some ways for my work. However, I am certain that nowhere in my education did we learn how to deal with diabolical cases. Those were just seen in movies or on television, not something we will encounter in our lifetime. We were taught spiritual warfare in terms of prayer and the devotion to the holy angels and the saints, but nothing academically prepared me for dealing with demonic conditions. I have to give credit to my parents for sharing with us their Catholic Faith and living a life of sacrifice and prayer as a testimony of God's presence among us. As a young child, our paraplegic mother led us to the holy rosary instilling a special devotion to the Mother of God, while our dad took us to church. We were encouraged to not only believe but to be involved in the profession and spreading of our faith. As such as a teenager, my twin sister and I became involved in the Legion of Mary in the Philippines and eventually I reconnected with the Legion here in the U.S.A. and became involved in the Diocese of Arlington. The powerful Dominican education I received in high school and college laid a strong foundation to the tenets of my Catholic Faith, which has been an integral part of my day to day living and rightfully, became an integral part of who I am as a clinician. In fact, one's spiritual belief is a stepping stone and a door in the discernment of clinical cases.

RELIGIOUS FOUNDATION

Is religion really important in one's life? To answer this question, I found this brief story which serves as an analogy and explains it well.

"There was an old fisherman who took a young man out in his small boat. The young man noticed that on one of the oars was written the word 'Prayer' and on the other 'Work.' "Well," said the youth, "that idea is all right for those who wish to depend on prayer, but it is out of date. Work is the thing needed in the world; we can get along without prayer and religion." The old man said nothing, but let go of the oar on which 'Prayer' was written, and rowed with the other. He rowed and rowed, but they only went around in a circle and made no progress. The youth understood the old fisherman's lesson: that besides the oar of 'Work' we also need the oar of 'Prayer.' Religion is necessary for all of us." (E. Hayes, 2002, p. 20)

A strong religious foundation is the backdrop for the discernment of diabolical conditions. It is hard to explain the spiritual conditions upon which to base one's experiences without having also a spiritual foundation to refer from. In the same way that we need physical light to see in the midst of physical darkness, we need spiritual light to see in the midst of spiritual darkness. How do we develop this spiritual light? It starts in the home.

The home is the first school of faith and the parents are the foremost educators of that faith. Living by example is very important in passing on the faith. As St. Francis said, "Preach all the time but only use words when necessary." Actions indeed speak louder than words. If parents pray everyday, do religious acts or devotions regularly, attend weekly or daily Masses, receive the sacraments of Penance monthly and Holy Communion weekly, attend religious retreats annually, read spiritually uplifting books, watch religious shows or movies, seek spiritual direction and live charitably both in words and actions, the children will observe these behaviors and apply them in their own personal lives.

I remember a family whom I saw in therapy because the teenagers were acting up. In meeting the family members, it was so evident that anger permeated their daily interaction. The father was extremely cruel, verbally abusive, a harsh disciplinarian, and ironically, a "devout Catholic." The mother was passive, insecure, and was not respected by any member of the family because she was disrespected by the father in front of the children. Sadly, the children said to me that when they reach 18, they planned to leave their horrible home and they had no plans of practicing their Catholic Faith. All they could remember were the constant criticisms of them before they left for church, related either to the way they combed their hair or the way they were attired, the constant rushing, and cursing on the way to church. "Hypocrites, such hypocrites," were the remarks of the teenagers. What a waste of time to spend the children's formation in constant tension and turmoil when parents can use valuable growing years of the children to affirm them and let them know of the true love of God for them.

St. Therese of Lisieux's parents, Louis Martin and Azelie Marie Guerin, are true examples of good parenting. They raised their five daughters in the faith. They prayed daily rosaries, taught them the Catholic Faith, observed religious festivities, integrated family fun activities, guided them by example, and enkindled in them the beauty of God's love, fidelity, and forgiveness. Not only did the five daughters enter the convent, but St. Thérèse was declared both a saint and a doctor of the Church. The Martins are considered a model of sanctity as a couple and were beatified in 2008. If families work together to enrich one another to grow in virtue, then children will have a better chance of growing up with a strong foundation in the Faith.

As an adult, every one has the responsibility to further grow in the faith handed on to him. It is not enough to have known one's faith. Reading more religious material, listening to live or recorded talks on spiritual matters, surrounding oneself with spiritually minded Catholic friends, daily prayers, visitation of the Blessed Sacrament in Catholic churches, frequent reception of the sacraments, and spiritual guidance are essential in growing in one's faith and truly being able to take ownership of that faith. All these are essential in becoming authentic Catholics and taking an adult ownership of one's Catholic Faith. If one does not grow, we will stagnate, dry up, and be sucked in by the secular world that will negate the very teachings one has learned as a child.

Everyone who has to deal with these difficult cases cannot be negligent of their spiritual state because one is treading on dangerous waters that require a ready life line. Here are some areas to consider in order to build on a strong religious foundation.

Prayer Life

All practitioners dealing with diabolical cases should have a strong prayer life. Begin each day with a quick prayer. For my fellow Catholics, may I suggest the Morning Offering, prayers of thanksgiving for a new day, prayer to your guardian angel, prayer to St. Michael the Archangel, prayer to our Blessed Virgin Mary & St. Joseph and asking God for direction in all undertakings. Ask for the Precious Blood of Jesus to cover you and your loved ones to be protected from all evil and all harm, including your vehicle and the buildings where you will be staying. During the day, consult with God in all your decisions. If you can pray the Liturgy of the Hour, joining the universal Church in prayer is great! Remember the Chaplet of Divine Mercy at 3:00 PM and always end you day with a night prayer thanking God for the help throughout the day and asking for forgiveness for any shortcomings. At night, make sure you are armed again with your holy angels and ask Jesus Christ's Precious Blood to protect you and your loved ones in your sleep, including the protection of your properties.

Frequent reception of the sacraments

The sacrament of Penance is a healing sacrament. Go regularly, at least monthly, and it will be nice to consult a holy priest who can become your confessor. Having a regular priest who gets to know you is good for humility and for guidance. Really take time to examine your conscience and be sincere in your contrition.

With a clean conscience, receive Our Lord frequently in Holy Communion. Imagine if you have in you the presence of Jesus Christ every day. You can have a direct line with God who listens to your prayers. Remember: He does not always give you what you want, but what you need. Remain faithful.

Frequent visits to the Blessed Sacrament

If you can not stay for Mass, at least you can say hello to Jesus on your way to or from work. It only takes a minute for you tell Him how much you love Him and how much you want Him to be a part of your life. If one has time to get much closer to God, then a holy hour before the Monstrance in a Perpetual Adoration Chapel or in front of the Tabernacle in every Catholic Church will be an appropriate response to Christ calling, "Can you spend an hour with Me?"

Active participation in a church ministry

If you do not immerse yourself into your Catholic Faith, you will find yourself superficially knowing very little about your faith. Sooner or later, the little you know will be eroded by materialism or sucked out by confusing ideologies of other competing beliefs. There are a number of ministries in every parish. One must search for the calling and participate actively in some form of ministry in order to develop a richer and fuller commitment to one's faith and a closer intimacy with God who is the true Teacher in dealing with these delicate cases. The only One who can effect the needed change and can perform the required miraculous healing is God. Jesus Christ who suffered, died, and resurrected from the dead is the Power and in His name, every knee shall bend on earth, under the earth, and beyond. Jesus Christ is Lord!

Continue to learn about your Catholic Faith

The available literature, CD's, cassette tapes, and videos are abundant. If you do not wish to purchase them, look at what is available to borrow in your parish. You may order free literature leaflets via the internet or mail. There are local Catholic libraries or county libraries where you may borrow such materials. Consult your priest friend or local pastor for recommended readings. Use your time wisely. Even travel time can be used to learn by putting on CD or cassette tape in your console so your commuting time is a time for education.

Seek spiritual direction

Finding a good spiritual director is crucial in one's discernment of cases. I suggest that a person makes a novena for the specific intention of finding a holy priest, deeply rooted in the Catholic faith, who is loyal to the Magisterium, for one's spiritual guide. Patience is needed in waiting for the right one. This may require diligence in going to confession for the time being to different priests until the inspiration comes that you have met the right one. Once you have one, meet monthly or as often as your spiritual director can accommodate in his schedule. Discuss with him your spiritual journey and areas you are struggling with.

Wear and use sacramentals

I recommend wearing the Miraculous Medal and the Brown scapular. We need the protection of our Heavenly Mother. It is imperative to wear a crucifix around one's neck and whenever you run into a problem, kiss your crucifix and ask God for guidance. Have a crucifix available in your offices. Better still, put one in every room. Have holy water, holy salt, and a Bible available. Have a rosary in your possession to use for prayer.

EDUCATIONAL FOUNDATION

Academically, everyone must continue to learn despite one's higher education. It is better to be a perpetual student, so to speak, in order to always make room for further learning. My seven years of doctoral work and two years of masters' work did not prepare me in dealing with diabolical cases. However, the knowledge I received and the extensive experience I gained allowed me to be able to discriminate first and rule out the type of psychiatric conditions that might be present before I could even entertain any sense of spiritual condition. In many cases, the co-morbidity is present. Many cases suffer from some form of psychiatric condition and also suffer from demonic attack. This makes sense since the evil one is looking for vulnerability, any door open for one to come in. The invitation was made open by the person, whether knowingly or unknowingly. We know of such cases when children are exposed by their parents or care takers to demonic or new age activities leading to exposure and unfortunate vulnerability.

Any professional in the medical field is expected to participate in continuing education in his or her respective field in order to ensure currency of clinical knowledge and clinical practice. Continuing education is a pre-requisite for keeping one's licensure or board certification.

After graduating from college, I did not want to go back to school. I thought I was done with school work. It was not even months after graduation when I felt a need to go back and pursue my masters' degree in order to advance in my field of study. As a nursing student, I had adequate knowledge of anatomy, physiology, pathophysiology, pharmacology, biochemistry, and medical interventions. However, I wanted to pursue the field of psychology since I was already working as a psychiatric-mental health nurse in a Catholic hospital. I was fortunate to have completed my nursing degree at the prestigious Pontifical University of Santo Tomas in the Philippines, the oldest Catholic university in Asia, so I also had tremendous knowledge in theology, logic, and apologetics based on the writings of St. Thomas Aquinas. By pursuing more studies in the field of psychology, I had a greater body of knowledge essential to the diagnosis and understanding of the human psyche. My studies were interrupted by my departure to the United States when the Philippines was under martial law and political upheaval was taking place back home. I felt called to do my further studies abroad, which led me to the Catholic University of America to pursue my masters' degree in Psychiatric-Mental Health Nursing, a decision that paid off since I received wonderful clinical and didactic lessons applicable to my field of practice. After going through a rigorous comprehensive exam, I developed pre-eclampsia and Bell's palsy at the last trimester of my pregnancy. I said that I was definitely done with schooling at that point, but God had a different plan. I received another calling to pursue my doctorate in the field of stress and pain management at the University of Maryland with an outstanding program on human psychophysiology, the interworking of the mind and the body. This program allowed me to have a strong foundation in how the mind affects the body and how the body affects the mind. This body of knowledge is critical in the clinical work of dealing with physical disease created by psychological stress, and, in turn, helping patients cope with the psychological distress created by the chronicity of a physical condition. The condition of the soul affects both the mind and the body.

In the same way that we can not allow ourselves to stagnate intellectually, we must be constantly vigilant to grow in our body of knowledge in order to become competent clinicians. Here are some things to pursue:

Attend educational conferences in your field

Every professional group sponsors continuing education programs, which help meet the required number of credits for license renewal. Every clinician must participate in such programs or conferences. The body of knowledge in the field is growing, if not mushrooming. The only way we can keep up with the changes is to continue learning.

Read books and literature related to your field of interest

The available textbooks, journals, and leaflets related to your work are abundant. Instead of reading entertainment books or magazines, which do not nurture the mind and soul, read available research and non-research materials instead, which can help understand the complexity of medical and psychological conditions. Many patients come with co-morbidities, so it is essential to be alert and to do a differential diagnosis.

Listen to available audio learning tapes or CD

If you do not have the time to read, then listen to available recorded materials. As mentioned previously, you can use travel time to enrich your mind and learn something new.

Take time to confer with colleagues in the field

If you are in a group practice, make use of the availability of your colleagues to discuss cases. If you do not have anyone in your group, take out a colleague to lunch and discuss important issues that may be bothersome to you. Get another person's perspective on how certain conditions are addressed by another person in your field. You may consider joining a listserv of people in the same field where you can discuss cases over e-mail.

Look up information on the internet

In this day and age, anyone can have a quick access to information via computers. If you have a multi-function cell phone or laptop, one can research drugs, diseases, or any related information at one's fingertips. It is amazing how valid and accurate information can be immediately available wherever you are without running to the nearest library. Look up reliable web sites to get the answer you are looking for, such as ones that are peer-reviewed or associated with recognized professional organizations, maintained by experienced clinicians whom you trust, or written by individuals with reputable religious affiliations.

Integration of Mind, Body and Spirit with God's Grace

With a good understanding of the human body, the psyche of the mind, and the spiritual nature of the human soul, we have the ammunition to better differentiate one condition from the other, namely, to be able to discriminate among psychological disorders, physical diseases, and spiritual conditions. Above all, the clinician is encouraged to have a deep prayer life and a daily sacramental life in order to hear the tiny whispers of God in our everyday encounters with patients to assist in our discernment of cases.

A well-balanced life is critical to functioning well on a day-to-day basis. It is not enough just to be learned. It is not enough to spend time in prayer. What we need is truly having God integrated in our daily lives. With this in mind, we need to grow in virtues—in fact, heroic virtues. This means the ability to practice virtues on a regular, consistent basis even when it may be difficult. "Human virtues are firm attitudes, stable dispositions, and habitual perfections of intellect and will that govern our actions, order our passions, and guide our conduct according to reason and faith. They make self-mastery and discipline in leading a morally good life not only possible, but even easy. The virtuous man is he who freely practices the good. The moral virtues are acquired by human effort and God's grace. They are the fruit and seed of consistent morally good acts; they dispose all the powers of the human being for communion with Divine Love." (Catechism of the Catholic Church [CCC], 1994, p. 443)

Here is a list of virtues to be developed to be effective as a clinician working for God and discerning problems that are spiritual in nature:

Humility is a supernatural virtue by which a Christian gains a proportionate and fitting understanding of one's relationship to God. Humility is truth. This virtue allows us to accept that everything good comes from God and is only made possible by the grace of God. We may accomplish beneficial or even phenomenal achievements. Let us remember the primary source of all good is God and He alone is the object of all these good deeds. If on a daily basis we offer our work, joys, and suffering for the love and service of God, we are starting our day with humility. Every time somebody praises our work or accomplishment, let us respond, "Thanks be to God," to show that it is only by the merits of His grace that we are able to accomplish these good works. Since humility is truth, we are not to downplay any compliments since that can be false humility and a failure to give a chance to praise our Creator. If we are not able to humble ourselves, we can be sure that God will find a way to humble us. When that happens, it is usually more painful rather than simply accepting what comes our way. We may even receive criticisms for the good that we do. Thank God for the opportunity to suffer with Him and to practice humility. We cannot for certain please everyone, let alone every patient. We must be sure that we please God above all. Let us work with humility knowing that we can be vessels of God's awesome powers.

Obedience is a supernatural virtue that allows a person to want to conform one's will to the will of God. The ultimate goal of obedience is to fulfill God's plan for us and to please God above all. This virtue is not easy to practice because our will seems to want to enforce itself to God as if we could "twist the arm" of God, so to speak. Our will collides with God's will. We want to be in control of everything. We think we know it all so we want things to happen our way. The truth is that God gave us free will to be exercised by us with prudence, so we should use this freedom to align it to God's loving Providence. He has no desire than for us to be truly free—free to get to Heaven. We accomplish this in abiding by the laws of God.

Charity is a theological virtue by which a person loves God, and out of that love flows the love of others for the love of God. This is the greatest of all virtues because from this virtue flows many others. Love is a powerful emotion that we can exercise properly to be able to do great things with love. Every servant of God should start the day telling God, "I love You." This can easily be said by making the sign of the cross upon awakening and looking at the crucifix, saying, "Good morning, God. I love You." This will not take but a second. We can then show this love of God to the people with whom we live and the people we work. Love is contagious. The more we love, the more people are drawn to us so we can draw them to God, our Beloved. Every patient that comes through the office is in need of love. There is so much emotional poverty around us. Lonely people are around us. Love is lacking in homes, in the community, and in our society. If every patient can experience the love of God by coming in contact with us, then we have done something good. Love is a powerful gift we can give to every patient by accepting them as children of God in need of our support and understanding. This degree of true charity may require sacrifice on our part, namely, out of love for God we may have to see patients at no charge since they are not only suffering from emotional poverty but from financial poverty. We can be true witnesses of Christian love to others.

Faith is a theological virtue by which we believe in God, in everything that God has revealed to us, and all that is taught to us by the Catholic Church because she teaches the truth, even when it is not easy to believe. Our senses help us to believe in things, but there are also things that are supernatural and imperceptible to the senses, but we believe because God has told us it is so, and God is truth. A "leap of faith" is required. The Church teaches us what to believe since these teachings within her repository are based both on Sacred Scripture and Sacred Tradition passed on from generation to generation. Faith allows us to believe things we do not understand, cannot comprehend, or are unable to prove. Christ said that if we have the faith the size of a mustard seed, we can tell a mountain to move (Matthew 17:20). Do we really know the size of a mustard seed? It is the size of a speck of dust. That is how little faith is required of us; the rest that is lacking in us will be delivered by God. Faith indeed moves mountains. Faith makes things possible that seem impossible. Faith is what is required for our part: God takes care of the rest. Let us ask God, "Lord, I wish to believe, help my unbelief" (Mark 9:24).

Hope is a theological virtue from God to be able to believe that we can make it to Heaven and that He will give us the strength to make it there. This grace gives us a yearning for happiness something we all aspire. Hope is so important in the midst of the depression around us. We have to be a voice of hope when everything seems to be hopeless, especially with diabolical cases. Our very presence with our patients and our willingness to be there and not give up on them can be a source of hope for them. Hope is believing that God is going to be there for us. The truth is that God is always faithful and is indeed always there for us. The problem tends to be with our faulty cooperation. We are the ones guilty of having turned away from Him. When we turn our backs to Him, we feel alone and far away. We can see Him if we take a moment to look back, because He is there waiting patiently for our return. God is constant. We are not. Nevertheless, He is a loving Father welcoming us when we are ready. Let us convey this hope to every patient.

Fortitude is a cardinal virtue and gift of the Holy Spirit that allows a person to persevere in the pursuit of good even in the midst of trials, difficulties, pain, and suffering. It allows a Christian to overcome obstacles in the course of doing the will of God. The society in which we live expects things to happen and happen quickly. We are in the "microwave age" when we must have results in a matter of minutes. Everything is happening at accelerated pace. Just as suddenly, though, we run into a wall: now what? This is the time to separate the heroes from the cowards. Heroes and heroines for God persevere in the midst of suffering. They are not afraid to persevere even if it means pain and suffering. We run the race (cf 1 Timothy 4:7) not for earthly laurels but for a golden crown that never fades in Heaven. That reward must be kept in mind to help us to persevere to the end. We need to pray for patience to persevere at all times.

Prudence is a gift of the Holy Spirit to know what is right from wrong and the ability to make the correct judgment. Wisdom is necessary in dealing with psychiatric conditions and even more so with diabolical conditions. As counselors, we are put in a position to help guide people to make the right decisions. This is a serious responsibility that will be impacting our patients not only in this life, but in the life to come. Souls are at stake. If our minds are clear from the clutter of the world and open to God's grace, then we can provide better guidance to these souls. We have to remember that every action has reactions and repercussions. No action is done in a vacuum. Every action affects others even though we claim that nobody knows or nobody will see it. We are a part of the Mystical Body of Christ: Christ is the Head and we are the parts of that same body. If we are a broken finger, then that pain can be felt by the rest of the body. Every decision we make affects others, whether we see or not. It is vital then to pray to the Holy Spirit for guidance so that we may have the prudence to choose what is right and pleasing to God.

Temperance is the "moral virtue that moderates the attraction of pleasures and provides balance in the use of created goods. It ensures the will's mastery over instincts and keeps desires within the limits of what is honorable. The temperate person directs the sensitive appetites toward what is good and maintains a healthy discretion." (CCC, p.445) With temperance, we are able to guide our patients to have a balance in life, to curb impulses, and avoid any excesses in the pursuit of pleasure or material goods. We all want to be happy. However, if we do not curtail our appetites, we can find ourselves completely overwhelmed, paradoxically empty from our consumption of the world and in financial and spiritual debt, far away from the happiness of being fulfilled in God.

Justice is the "moral virtue that consists of the constant and firm will to give proper due to God and neighbor. Justice toward God is to give Him the time in prayer that God deserves, the daily practice of what is good and use of talents that give glory to God. Justice towards men disposes one to respect the rights of each and to establish harmony in human relationships that promotes equity with regard to persons and to the common good. The just man, often mentioned in sacred Scripture, is distinguished by habitual right thinking and the uprightness of his conduct toward his neighbor" (CCC, p. 444). Often we are consulted by a patient as to what is a just response or action to be taken in response to an act of injustice received by that person. In giving advice, we must remember that mercy is greater than justice. We must apply justice tempered with mercy for others.

Understanding is a gift of the Holy Spirit which St. Thomas Aquinas said: "to give a deeper insight and penetration of divine truths held by faith, not as a transitory enlightenment but as a permanent intuition. Illuminating the mind to truth, the Holy Spirit aids a person to grasp truths of faith easily and intimately. In this very life, when the eye of the spirit is purified by the gift of understanding, one can in a certain way see God." (Summa Theologica, 1952, pp. 416-422)

In the field of psychology, patients often consult us in understanding what is really going on in their lives and the meaning of their particular situation. We are forced to brighten the light of illumination so we can clearly see the crux of the matter in the eyes of God. We must be able to see the truth in light of God's truth. Sometimes even though we present the truth, this can be hard to take because people may not be ready or be willing to see. However, we must be a voice of truth to the people we counsel.

Counsel is a gift of the Holy Spirit to render the individual docile and receptive to the counsel of God regarding one's actions in view of one's sanctification and salvation. Primarily, this gift enables a person to judge individual acts as good and necessary to do, or as evil and necessary to avoid. The role of a counselor is indeed serious and carries a hefty prize since our advice has ramifications towards the salvation of one's soul and the soul of the patient being guided. Undeniably, the role of a counselor is to guide the client to become whole, holy and be brought closer to God, his Creator.

Knowledge is the gift that enables a person "to judge rightly concerning the truths of faith in accordance with their proper causes and the principles of revealed truth. Under the guidance of the Holy Spirit, the human intellect makes correct judgments regarding earthly things and how they are related to eternal life and Christian perfection. This gift enables us to realize the emptiness of created things so that they do not become roadblocks to union with God. At the same time, it enables us to see through created things to the God who created them. Therefore, instead of seeing all created things as obstacles to union with God, we can view them as instruments we can use to achieve our union with God. As such, every client can see how to use created things rightly and responsibly. In the same way, we as counselors have to grow in knowledge of how we can use our work to further the purpose of God for His creatures, namely, on how we can be instruments of God to bring souls to Heaven." (Summa Theologica, 1952, pp. 423-425)

If a clinician is serious about being able to properly discern the presence of diabolical conditions, this chapter must be re-read and taken into account because there is no easy way to prepare a clinician to deal with the horrors of diabolical possession. It takes grace from God to be able to have the courage to face such hideous clients, something every clinician would wish not to encounter, but it happens. When it does, that mental health provider will have the ability to tackle the job on hand.

PRAYER AND HEALING:
FAITH AND SCIENCE UNITE

"We must pray without tiring, for the salvation of mankind does not depend on material success; nor on sciences that cloud the intellect. Neither does it depend on arms and human industries, but on Jesus alone."

—St. Frances Xavier Cabrini

CHAPTER 12

Prayer and Healing:
Faith and Science Unite

The longing for happiness, deeply rooted in the human heart, has always been accompanied by a desire to be freed from illness and to be able to understand the meaning of sickness when it is experienced. This is a human phenomenon, which in some way concerns every person and finds particular resonance in the Church, where sickness is understood as a means of union with Christ and of spiritual purification (Purgatory here on earth). Moreover, for those who find themselves in the presence of a sick person, it is an occasion for the exercise of charity and compassion. Sickness, like other forms of human suffering, is a privileged moment for prayer whether asking for grace, the ability to accept sickness in a spirit of faith and conformity to God's will, or to ask for healing. Prayer for the restoration of health is therefore part of the Church's experience in every age, including our own. Prayer is an effective and powerful tool to assist us in our healing. Prayer aligns our will to God's will. The power of our faith put into action, prayer delivers the most unexpected, the most miraculous results that boggle the most brilliant minds of our scientific society.

I was one of the recipients of such healing, revealing the power of faith. In the year 2000, I was very sick and weak. Earlier in the year, I was diagnosed with pneumonia and had to be on antibiotics. I was bedridden. Weeks passed and the pneumonia was healed, but I remained weak with no energy. Something was happening since there were remarkable changes in my left breast and I had a lump in my left armpit (axilla). I realized the signs of cancer and I did not know what to do. If I said something to my family, I would be forced to seek medical assistance. However, we were previously scheduled to go to a pilgrimage to Fatima, Portugal, so I thought to myself I only had to wait for that time. In my prayers, I asked God for prudence. Should I go now for treatment or should I wait? Something inside me said, "Do you have enough faith?" My answer to that was, "I do." I made a deal with God that if He chose not to heal me, I would be obedient and would call my doctor who would refer me to an oncologist. If God in His infinite power and majesty chose to heal me, then I choose to be a witness to the world of His awesome goodness and mercy. May came around and we flew to Portugal. I was very excited to attend the evening Eucharistic procession and we sang praises to God. The following morning after my shower, I realized that my left breast looked normal again and the lump in my armpit was gone. "Blessed be God!" I exclaimed the glory and power of God! I remained silent about the entire miraculous healing and attended the Eucharistic procession the following night, thanking God for my miraculous healing. By Sunday morning after going to Mass, we sat down for breakfast and I shared my miraculous healing to my family. They were so surprised since they did not know anything about it and relieved for my gift. On the other hand, they were angry that I did not say anything before that. They were as happy as I felt praising God for my miraculous cure. Indeed, praise the Lord!

What is this place called Fatima where my miraculous healing took place? To millions of people, Fatima is a place of healing, like Lourdes in France. Our Blessed Virgin Mary appeared to these three little shepherds as they pastured their sheep. Our Lady revealed to these innocent souls such horrific secrets. In addition, they were given a chance to see what hell was like, what purgatory was like, and what Heaven was like. The people of Fatima had mixed responses. Those desperate for miracles were quickly trailing these children, while the cynical were watching from a distance questioning the irrational beliefs of the faithful and finding ways to obstruct this so called embarrassing madness of their town, which had become the laughing stock of their nation, Portugal. On October 13, 1917, the great miracle of the sun took place in the presence of thousands of pilgrims. The sun became gloriously colorful in the middle of a rainy day and appeared to come out of orbit as if it were going to plunge directly towards earth. The people panicked and begged God for mercy as they ran for their lives. When it ended, their clothes were totally dry and the entire location had no sign of the soaking rain and mud, in which they were treading earlier. Despite all the newspaper reporters focused on this miraculous occasion, not all were convinced. No miracle happened for them. For the believers, miraculous healings took place.

We are finicky people. We want miracles but do not ask for one. Even if we ask, we do not have faith that it can happen to us. We instead rely on all the gadgets and technologies available to us for a hefty cost rather than ask God in prayer that does not cost us a dime. All it takes is a leap of faith. What happened to us? We are in the 21st century with all the imaginable advancements in medicine, in science, telecommunications, and in technology. Just look around us. We have the most towering buildings reaching up to the skies. We have space shuttles that have landed on the moon. We have satellite information bridging the gap between continents. We have all the technologically advanced forms of communication. At our fingertips are hand-held computers, cell phones, GPS, and internet service. We can call long distance or make local calls all for the same price. We can connect so far away and see each other using digital communication. With our ability to connect with others on so many levels, why are we still miserable?

The answer to this is very simple. We do not have God in our hearts and in our minds. If we totally believe that Christ is visibly present in every tabernacle in the world, we should have all the churches packed with people in and out of our churches to pray and communicate with God. He is there simply waiting for us. If we truly believe that in every Holy Communion, Christ is present in His Body, Blood, Soul, and Divinity, should we not approach Him with such reverence and believe that He can make anything possible?

You may have heard the saying: Whatever the mind can conceive and believe with the help of God, we can achieve. God will never impose His will on us. We must desire to do His will. We must believe that God is omnipotent and omniscient. We can never ever be close enough in our limited human power compared to the divine majesty of God. We presume too much that whatever we desire is what is best for us. We want to control everything. God knows what is best for us. Trust in Him. Believe in Him. Miracles do happen.

In the most widely publicized studies of the effect of intercessory prayer, cardiologist Randolph Byrd studied 393 patients admitted to the coronary-care unit at San Francisco General Hospital in 1986. Some were prayed for by home-prayer groups, others were not. All the men and women received medical care. In this randomized, double-blind study, neither the doctors and nurses nor the patients knew who would be the object of prayer. The results were dramatic and surprised many scientists. The men and women whose medical care was supplemented with prayer needed fewer drugs and spent less time on ventilators. They also fared better overall than their counterparts who received medical care but nothing more. The prayed-for patients had significantly less need for antibiotics and less likely to develop complications.

In another double blind study done in 1998, Dr. Elisabeth Targ and her colleagues at California Pacific Medical Center in San Francisco showed the benefits of prayer on patients with advanced AIDS. Their findings showed that those patients receiving prayer survived in greater numbers, got sick less often, and recovered faster than those not receiving prayer.

"Prayer works," says Dr. Dale Matthews, who practices internal medicine and teaches at the Georgetown University School of Medicine in Washington, D.C., has reviewed more than 200 studies linking religious commitment and health, cited in his book, *"The Faith Factor."* Dr. Matthews cites studies suggesting that people who pray are less likely to get sick, are more likely to recover from surgery and illness and are better able to cope with their illnesses than people who don't pray. Some evidence indicates that sick people who are prayed for also fare significantly better than those who are not the recipients of prayer. In fact, some physicians report that people who are prayed for often do better even if they don't know somebody is praying for them.

In his book *"God, Faith, and Health: Exploring the Spiritual-Healing Connection,"* Dr. Jeff Levin reports the findings of hundreds of academic studies connecting religious faith with medical benefits. He cites a study done by California's respected Human Population Laboratory, which tracked 5,000 people for 28 years and found that those who frequently attended church were 23 percent less likely to die during the study period than people who did not regularly go to church. He also notes that a deeply held religious faith seems to be particularly effective in warding off death among people who are already ill or infirm and wish to return to good health. The researchers at Dartmouth

Medical School examined the survival rates of 232 post-surgical cardiac patients. "Deaths in a six-month follow-up period after open-heart surgery were 11 percent in patients who considered themselves 'not at all,' 'slightly' or 'fairly religious,' Dr. Levin reported." "In those who were 'deeply' religious, the death rate was zero."

Faith and science can complement each other as proven by the above-mentioned researches. God is the author of life and the Cause of these observable effects. Our faith as practiced in prayer for others can create miraculous healings as seen in my practice and evidenced in the results of aforementioned studies. Here are a few words to help every clinician to remember to make prayer a part of their lives and to encourage prayer among their patients, which can be summarized in the acronym FAITH.

F: Faith in Divine Providence

Jesus asks us to be cautious but not unbelieving (Mark 13:23). He was deeply hurt one day when the father of an epileptic demoniac said, "If you can do anything, have pity on us and help us." "If you can?" retorted Jesus. "Everything is possible to anyone who has faith." Immediately the father of the boy cried out, "I do have faith. Help the little faith I have!" (Mark 9:23)

The miracles Jesus worked were not so much acts of mercy as signs that He is the Son of God. They were directed towards increasing the faith of both recipient and onlooker. They were symbolic of the messianic age, the coming of the kingdom and the power of the Spirit. When these ends were not accomplished, Jesus worked no miracles. It was for this reason He worked so few in His own home town.

The prayer of the Christian is always answered: sometimes it is "yes," sometimes it is "no," or sometimes it is "not yet." Christian prayer is to be made in faith and that faith gives one the humble detachment so necessary to move the mountains of doubt. One should never question God's love when His answer is "no." The Faith of the Christian sees God's Love in every event of his life.

A: Abandonment to God's Plan

This act of humility, of acceptance of God's will, was the spirit Jesus desired before His power reached out and touched those in need: the deeper the faith, the greater the humility. The centurion, who asked Jesus to heal his servant, said, "Sir, I am not worthy to have you under my roof. Just give the word and my servant shall be cured." No wonder Jesus said, "I tell you solemnly, nowhere in Israel have I found faith like this" (Matthew 8:8). This beautiful act of trust and self-abandonment on the part of the centurion touched the Heart of Jesus. This man believed Jesus was the Son of God, one so powerful that an act of His Will could accomplish the miraculous. The man humbly waited: "Just give the word," he said and all would be well. Jesus' followers are to grow in Faith by adherence to the Father's Will and by carrying the cross His love placed upon them.

We can humbly pray for what we need, be it physical, material or temporal, knowing that our Father is God and is powerful enough to give us whatever we ask, provided it is for our good. Humility enables us to admit we do not always know in what that good consists.

I: Imitation of the Saints

The Holy Cross Brother, known as "Frère Andre," has been credited with thousands of cures. The recently canonized St. Andre was the founder of St. Joseph's Oratory in Montreal, Canada, perhaps the world's principal shrine in honor of St. Joseph. If one were to seek the outstanding virtue of Brother Andre one would have to say that it was his humility. He once said, "I am ignorant. If there were anyone more ignorant, the good God would choose him in my place." When the power of healing was attributed to him, he corrected them that it was St. Joseph who helped them. The saints are obedient, humble, charitable, and resigned to the will of God. They accept whatever God has in store for each of them. The saints unite their sufferings to the sufferings of Christ on the Cross. They too experience doubts and fears sometimes, but in the end, they attain peace and resignation to God's plan.

T: Think Positively

Every experience is picked up by the senses and transferred to the brain for interpretation. This brief second of interpretation is crucial to our well-being. If we tend to interpret things negatively, we alert the alarm system of the body to initiate a stress reaction. This means that hormones are flooding our system which, if not used, cause negative effects in our body, that is, the breakdown of cells causing illnesses. If however, we decided to make a positive interpretation of the incident, then the body is relaxed and the mind is more open to possibilities. Positive thinking yields tremendous benefits in overcoming psychological conditions, for which reason I use cognitive therapy in psychotherapy.

H: Healthy Lifestyle

If we choose to sit in front of the television or the computer, then our fingers receive the exercise and our brains remain somewhat stagnant. We also have a choice of putting on our sneakers and taking brisk walks or jogging, which can improve our mood, lift the depression, control anxiety, and even control mania. The choice is ours. We have to recommend physical exercise to every patient.

We can choose to eat well and control diabetes mellitus, hypertension, anxiety, depression, or whatever medical illness we may have. However, daily temptations are before us. We can not seem to overlook desserts or sodas or the frequent trips to fast food restaurants for convenience.

We can decide to play video games all night and lose sleep while neglecting our family members, or we can be home with our family getting a good night's sleep so we can be rested and recovered.

We can rush every place we go or we can take the time to plan ahead, set priorities, and arrive on time at ease. Rushing not only predisposes us to accidents and making mistakes, but creates an alarm reaction in the body, starting a stress response. Let us take time to breathe and enjoy God's creation around us.

To sum up the interconnection of faith and science, I wish to quote a passage from the Catechism of the Catholic Church. "Though faith is above reason, there can never be any real discrepancy between faith and reason. Since the same God who reveals mysteries and infuses faith has bestowed the light of reason on the human mind, God cannot deny himself, nor can truth ever contradict truth." (Dei Filius 4: DS 3017) "Consequently, methodical research in all branches of knowledge, provided it is carried out in a truly scientific manner and does not override moral laws, can never conflict with the faith, because the things of the world and the things of faith derive from the same God. The humble and persevering investigator of the secrets of nature is being led, as it were, by the hand of God in spite of himself, for it is God, the conserver of all things, who made them what they are." (CCC, 1994, p. 43)

DIABOLICAL CONDITIONS:
A CLINICIAN'S FINAL REFLECTIONS

"Listen and attend with the ear of your heart."

—St. Benedict of Nursia

CHAPTER 13

DIABOLICAL CONDITIONS:
A CLINICIAN'S FINAL REFLECTIONS

The initial reactions of every practitioner who runs into diabolical conditions include fear and withdrawal. These natural responses are to be expected as defense mechanisms to something that confronts a practitioner without any warning in a mysterious and overpowering way. The enemy is invisible and supernatural. After seeing numerous cases and with prayerful discernment, one develops confidence and spiritual courage which makes facing such cases more manageable. Every case is unique and may elicit a different reaction from the clinician.

How long does it take before a clinician becomes familiar with diagnosing a diabolical condition from a psychological condition? Like anything else in life, time is the factor. With more exposures to such cases, the clinician is able to distinguish a demonic possession from a psychiatric condition. Another important element that needs to be emphasized is the strong role of spiritual growth on the part of the clinician. As the practitioner becomes spiritually mature, grace abounds and the ability to discriminate these cases also improves. This gift from God is a true blessing because it gives the practitioner a set of "clinical eyes" that helps the clinician to separate the psychological from the diabolical. Many cases are not clearly diabolical only. A majority of the cases I have seen have an underlying psychological condition in addition to having a demonic condition. In fact, this co-morbidity is what complicates the diagnosis particularly if there is a personality disorder, biochemical imbalance, or substance abuse. Which one came first? It is hard to say. My observation indicates several possibilities: pre-existing psychological conditions that predisposed the individual to pursue activities that made them more vulnerable to attacks, a family history which made them vulnerable, still others who made poor choices that led them to be exposed to the occult, and others who developed a psychological condition after being pursued by these relentless demonic spirits, leading them to feel helpless and hopeless. Every clinician must look for a "door" or "doors" that has or have opened to the patient and rendered the patient vulnerable to the attacks of the evil one. These so-called "doors" need to be examined closely in order to reduce recurring attacks and to prevent further attacks which can bring peace into the life of the patient and his family. Here are a few things to consider in examining "opened doors": pursue and look into family histories, past diabolical activities, associations with individuals who are involved with the occult or the New Age, and current activities of the client.

At the present time, there is no training available to mental health and medical professionals who may have to encounter such complex cases. The clergy have conferences or training that they can attend, but lay people have to learn "by fire"—direct contact with such cases. The best thing for a practitioner to do is to read about this subject matter and confer with those who have already seen such cases. Approaching a clergy, priest, religious, or even a lay person who may have already encountered such cases can be extremely helpful. The guidance of such individuals can help in the clinician's spiritual development, which in turn can be beneficial in developing spiritual discernment that comes only with a deep prayer life.

It is critical that clinicians find means to support each other and learn from each other. Since this is a very unique field, a clinician might feel alone and isolated. Having other people to confer with on this subject matter is also encouraged. It is indeed a challenge in this highly empirical, technological environment to describe an immaterial phenomenon and attempt to put it in a physical, material form when we are indeed dealing with a spiritual matter. In writing this manuscript, I hope that the following outcomes will become the fruits of having read this book:

- increase awareness and recognition of the presence of diabolical conditions

- develop a standardized diabolical interview
- use the tools provided in the last chapter to collect adequate data to develop a highly valid and reliable diagnostic instrument for clinical use
- gain confidence in dealing with such cases so that the people who suffer from these afflictions may receive adequate help with dignity and respect
- provide a forum for communication and support for the mental health and medical professionals
- design and provide annual training and conferences for both the laity and religious

Having participated in grand rounds in psychiatric hospitals, I listened to the agreements and disagreement of psychiatrists concerning the final diagnosis of our patients. One thing was for certain: if there were five psychiatrists in that room, there could be as many diagnostic conclusions in the end. In presenting the aforementioned cases, I hope I was able to elicit interest for all clinicians to discuss these cases, dissect them, and come up with their own differential diagnosis. I do not wish to imply that my conclusion is the only possible conclusion. By providing numerous case studies, I would like for practitioners to discuss them among themselves and use these cases as teaching tools for learning.

After reviewing the cases in chapters 6-9, answer the following questions:

1. What diagnostic work-up would you incorporate to further rule out and confirm your diagnosis?
2. What will be your final diagnosis for each of the cases?
3. What are the key signs and symptoms to support your answer?
4. How differently would you approach these cases?
5. What would you recommend to manage and treat these cases?

Each one of us is a student in this field. We have a perfect opportunity to bridge these spiritual cases with research so that in the end, we have served our community well in reducing the gap between science and religion. Let us take up the challenge and face evil with faith. In the end, no matter how smart we are or how many books we read, the bottom line is God. He is the true Healer and He alone has the power, authority, and dominion over the evil one.

GOD'S HEALING POWER:
A TESTIMONY OF FAITH

"Go forth in peace, for you have followed the good road. Go forth without fear, for he who created you has made you holy, has always protected you, and loves you as a mother. Blessed be you, my God, for having created me"

—St. Clare of Assisi

CHAPTER 14

GOD'S HEALING POWER:
A TESTIMONY OF FAITH

After ruling out the psychiatric conditions and the decision is made that the client suffers from a diabolical condition, then it is imperative to bring out the power behind any successful exorcisms—God Himself. He is the True Healer and it is imperative for any clinician to acknowledge that if a mental health worker intends to deal with possession cases in his practice, that professional better be armed with faith because the ride can be more treacherous than the wildest roller-coaster. As described in the previous chapter, to the practitioner armed with Faith, healing is possible because nothing is impossible with God. "Indeed as far as the Christian exorcist is concerned, it is not he or she who successfully completes the process; it is God who does the healing. The whole purpose of prayer and the ritual is to bring the power of God into the fray." (S. Peck, 1997, p. 186) A clinician must acknowledge that Jesus Christ is the only Savior and Mediator between man and God.

"Long live Christ the King! Viva Cristo Rey!"(Ball, 1996). These were the last words of Blessed Miguel Pro before the volley of shots echoed around him and his poor body was riddled with bullets. What a heroic act in the face of death! What a witness of faith for the hundreds who came to watch the event, to the thousands who read the newspaper, and thereafter, to the millions who have come to know and admire him. As for the rest of the world in these changing times, his voice echoes the truth. Christ is the Son of God and our Savior! He is the King of Kings. This scene came to mind with the recent feast of Christ the King, ending the liturgical year. I asked myself, "Who is your king?" Unequivocally, my response is that God is my only King and I choose to serve Him alone. This is important for us to reflect upon as we work with these delicate and challenging cases. No matter how smart we are or how many books we read, the bottom line is God is the True Healer and He alone has the power, authority, and dominion over the evil one.

With the current lack of fervor in the faith, when people are more concerned about more knowledge, more technology, more money, more power, and more sex, rather than saving their souls, the problems with the diabolical conditions will be on the rise. If God is not in our lives, I am positive that the evil one, who is roaring like a lion looking for a prey and does not sleep, will accrue many casualties. Faith is a gift from God. We have to nurture it and own it so that we can benefit from it. Often many self-serving people think that God is there to give them what they want and to respond to their every whim, so if God does not deliver, He is no longer important to them, which may even lead to their denial of God's existence. Faith helps us see the invisible, believe the incredible, and receive the impossible. I am a recipient of such a miraculous faith.

With the number of diabolical cases I saw in the past twenty years, I can not deny that no medication, no therapy can replace the HOLY NAME OF JESUS CHRIST. He alone can release these possessed patients from the grip of the evil one. No matter how I am challenged by some who believe that possession is left in the Middle Ages and is no longer the case in the our modern age and that these are simply psychotic patients who need good psychiatric treatment, I remain convinced by what I have seen and experienced, having seen both the devastation of evil and how it can be vanquished by the redeeming power of God. There has not been, nor can there ever be, a powerful enough medication to treat these diabolical cases, no matter how sophisticated and improved the psychotropic medications are now. God is the only answer.

We need to wake up from our materialistic mentality that there has to be something created by man that can handle these diabolical cases. We must stop and think. We are dealing with spiritual and diabolical situations wherein we cannot even see the enemy. All we see are the effects of evil on this person.

As a result, we need to use supernatural means in dealing with a supernatural event.

Jesus Christ is given the power and authority by the Heavenly Father to have dominion over all the principalities and powers; namely, over all angels, be it the good angels who remain faithful in the service of God or the bad angels who rebelled against God. I have witnessed the power of the Holy Eucharist, the real presence of our Lord Jesus Christ in the world. As I mentioned earlier in the book, I was miraculously healed from cancer during the Eucharistic procession in Fatima, Portugal. I also have seen patients dread the presence of the Holy Eucharist because the evil one recognizes the presence of our awesome God right before them. In the presence of the Holy Eucharist I witnessed a patient be released from the grip of the evil one.

We have many documented Eucharistic miracles throughout the world. (Lord, 2009) The oldest and the most scientifically studied miracle is the Eucharistic miracle of Lanciano in Lanciano, Italy. Right in this small Adriatic town is a miracle preserved by God for 1,300 years so that pilgrims may have a chance to renew their faith that God really means it when He said, "I shall be with you until the end of times" (Matthew 28:20). God never fails. God delivers and is faithfully present in all the tabernacles in every Catholic Church throughout the world. The Lanciano Eucharistic Miracle was put to a series of tests by scientists who did not believe that this was real and wanted to use modern technology to prove their point. I had a blessed opportunity to see for myself this wonderful miracle. Here is again the battle between faith and science. After rigorous studies of both the Sacred Host and the Precious Blood, their findings were:

- There was no evidence of preservative in these particles studied.
- The Sacred Host was found to be a piece of the human heart muscle (myocardium), which was thinly sliced in the most unique way imaginable and impossible to man, even with the most sophisticated laser equipment available. The muscle was as fresh as a newly excised tissue with all the elements of a fresh tissue intact. The Sacred Blood globule was liquefied and found to be as fresh as if it was just donated by someone. The blood is type AB and all the nutrients and minerals were actively present. (Lord, 2009).

Instead of disproving this well known miracle approved by the Catholic Church, the scientists were amazed, perplexed, and converted. God was vindicated from the arrogant and the intellectuals.

When Jesus Christ returns, will there still be people left with faith? (Luke 18:8). Let us affirm our faith in God. If we are going to work with these diabolical cases, we need God on our side. Let us renew our fidelity to God by attending Mass weekly or even daily. We must return to the sacrament of penance so we can receive our Lord Jesus Christ reverently in Holy Communion. With God within us, who can be against us? (Romans 8: 28-31). Who can defend us better than the way God can defend us? I have received many death threats in my years of clinical practice, but I keep going. We cannot live in fear. We must live in faith because God is in control and in charge of our lives. Our ultimate goal is to be holy and be united intimately with God because we are destined for Heaven. God is the Author of Life. God has the power to take away our life. God's power reigns for all eternity. He is the Alpha. He is the Omega (Revelations 1:8).

CHAPTER 15

APPENDICES

APPENDIX A

PROTECTION PRAYERS
PROTECTION AND HEALING PRAYER

Rev. Bob Hiltz, TOR
Healing and Deliverance Conference
Franciscan University, Steubenville, Ohio

Heavenly Father, I praise and thank You for all You have given me. Please cover me with the protective Precious Blood of Your Son, Jesus Christ, and increase Your Holy Spirit in me with His gifts of Wisdom, Knowledge, Understanding, Hunger for Prayer, Guidance, and Discernment to help me know Your will and surrender to it more completely.

Father, I forgive and ask forgiveness for my sins and failings, and ask that my whole person: body and mind, heart and will, soul and spirit, memory and emotions, attitudes and values be cleansed, renewed and protected by the Most Precious Blood of Your Son, Jesus Christ.

Father, please heal my negative emotions and any wounds in my heart and spirit. Send the sword of Your Holy Spirit to break all spells, curses, voodoo, and all negative, genetic, intergenerational and addictive material: past, present and future, known or unknown, against me, my ministry, finances and possessions, relationships and family.

In the Name, Power, Blood and Authority of Jesus Christ, I bind and break the power and effect in me of any and all evil spirits including those in the fire, air, earth, and water who are trying to harm me in any way and I command these spirits and their companion spirits to leave me quietly and peacefully and go immediately and directly to the Eucharistic presence of Jesus Christ in the closest Catholic Church tabernacle to be disposed of by Jesus and never again return to harm me. Jesus, please heal the effects of these spirits in myself and my life.

Dear Holy Spirit, please fill up any void in me to overflowing with Your great love. All these Father I pray in the name of Jesus Christ, Your Son and my Saving Lord by the guidance of Your Holy Spirit.

Immaculate Heart of Mary, Spouse of the Holy Spirit, please pray for and with me. Amen.

Note: Fr. Bob Hiltz TOR (1995) recommends praying this every morning and evening, followed by three Our Fathers. Please copy and give away.

PRAYER TO ST. MICHAEL THE ARCHANGEL

St. Michael the Archangel defend us in our battles, be our protection against the wickedness and snares of the devil. May God rebuke him we humbly pray. O thou Prince of the Heavenly Hosts, by the Power of God, cast into hell Satan and all his evil spirits who prowl about the world seeking the ruin of souls. Amen.

I recommend the prayer booklet published by Robert Abel on *Spiritual Warfare* for various prayers for personal protection from evil and for intergenerational healing.

APPENDIX B

Occult Exposure Questionnaire

©2012 Dr. Segunda Yanez Acosta

How vulnerable are you? Have you or has someone in your family:

Y N   Played with a Ouija board?

Y N   Played with Dungeons and Dragons, Magic the Gathering cards or other occult games?

Y N   Consulted a psychic?

Y N   Consulted a palm reader?

Y N   Sought the help of a channeler, spiritist, or medium?

Y N   Participated in witchcraft or got involved with witches?

Y N   Got involved in the black mass or devil worship?

Y N   Joined Freemasonry?

Y N   Made an oath to an anti-God organization?

Y N   Believed in horoscopes or astrology?

Y N   Enjoyed watching TV, movies, videogames or books with horror or evil thriller themes?

Y N   Been involved in satanic activities?

Y N   Collected charms and crystals believed to have powers or involved in crystal gazing?

Y N   Kept antiques or collectibles from other countries that have been used in pagan worship?

Y N   Participated in "healing services" invoking the devil?

Y N   Consulted a tarot card reader?

Y N   Obsessed with magical or unexplainable phenomena of the dark side?

Y N   Have an attraction to evil because it is forbidden?

Y N   Used the internet, cell phone, or other technologies for evil purposes?

Y N   Lived in a house where previous residents were involved in the occult?

Y N   Lived in a property where something tragic occurred in the past?

Y N   Lived in a property that was once used for evil purpose, e.g., prostitution or séances?

APPENDIX C

PSYCHOLOGICAL ASSESSMENT

The following conditions are not meant to be a complete listing of all psychiatric conditions. However, for the purpose of the psychological conditions that were addressed in the earlier cases, let us define certain psychiatric illnesses. Here are the definitions, signs and symptoms of the following conditions:

Major Depression is a mood disorder characterized by interference in the person's ability to function at home, at work, or wherever the person may be. The person demonstrates lack of joy and interest in life. The condition may be biochemical, also called endogenous depression or reactive depression induced by major changes in the person's life. The following signs and symptoms may be present:

- Persistent sadness, lost of joy, or feeling down
- Speech and movement are slow
- Speech content is self-deprecatory
- Sense of hopelessness, helplessness, and pessimism
- Tearfulness or crying with no provocation
- Lost of interest in activities that used to be important to the individual
- Lack of energy and constant complaint of fatigue
- Sleep disturbance, which includes either the inability to have good, quality sleep or sleeping too much, but waking up tired & not rested
- Irritability, agitation, or restlessness
- Withdrawal from others or isolating self
- Suicidal thoughts

Psychotic Depression is a severe form of depression wherein the individual's signs and symptom are exaggerated and accompanied by delusions or hallucinations. The person has disordered and disorganized thinking. The patient is aware of being depressed but cannot help it and may totally withdraw, in addition to saying or doing things that are not in touch with reality. This condition requires immediate attention because of the danger of self-harm. If the patient refuses to make a contract not to harm oneself and is determined to carry out those suicidal plans, this person needs immediate hospitalization.

Bipolar is a biochemical mood disorder characterized by highs and lows in moods and energy. It is also known as manic-depressive disorder, though this is an older term for the disorder. The patient usually vacillates between these two states, ranging from the zenith of mania including, but not limited to, unexplainable and extreme talkativeness, joy, over-excitement, rapid movements to the extreme explosive behavior of anger or rage to the nadir of depression, including lack of energy, motivation or interest.

Mania may be manifested as:

- Rapid, pressured speech
- Fast movements, rushing, hyperactive
- Insomnia or little sleep but retaining the ability to function
- Irritability, anger, periods of rages or melt-downs
- Excessive spending, desire for excitement, even to the point of high risk
- Racing thoughts, difficulty concentrating and focusing
- Moody; people around this person have to "walk on eggshells"
- Grandiosity or inflated self-worth
- Increased talkativeness; may or may not have flight of ideas
- Extremely animated facial expression, laughing uncontrollably

Psychotic Mania is a severe form of this condition that requires immediate attention since this can lead to self-harm or harm to others. The individual is so out of touch with reality that delusions and/or hallucinations are present. There is extreme agitation. The person has disorganized and disordered thinking and can become aggressive, violent and out of control which may require hospitalization.

Depression may be manifested as:

- Persistent sadness or gloominess
- Crying spells, including tearfulness without provocation
- Sleeping too much or being sluggish
- Often tired with loss of energy
- No motivation or interest to do anything
- Pessimistic, helpless, hopeless, worthless
- Withdrawn and isolated

- Psychomotor retardation
- Recurrent suicidal ideation
- May show agitated depression

Anxiety or generalized anxiety disorder is a condition that is characterized by chronic worrying, exaggerated tension, with little or no provocation. The following signs and symptoms may be present:

- Inability to stop worrying, "making mountains out of molehills"
- Trembling, shaking or appearing nervous
- Muscle tension, aches and pains without diagnostic findings
- Feeling overwhelmed and trapped
- Feeling out of control with life and unable to function
- Rapid heart rate, palpitations, tightness in the chest, hyperventilation
- Sweaty hands (profuse diaphoresis) or wringing of hands
- Feeling of uncertainty or uneasiness
- Pacing or constantly changing positions
- Enlarged pupils with furrowed brow

Obsessive-Compulsive Disorder is an anxiety disorder characterized by a recurrent, pressing, persistent thought process about a particular preoccupation, which becomes the obsession, followed by irresistible, repetitive behavior to respond to the thoughts, which become the compulsions. The signs and symptoms may include the following:

Obsessiveness may manifest as:

- Persistent, repetitive thoughts that are hard to dismiss and creates anxiety
- Ruminating over distressing thoughts
- Persistent scrupulosity
- Preoccupied with sequencing of numbers
- Frequently second-guessing oneself; self-doubt
- Feeling responsible for bad things happening around them
- Extreme guilt with excessive worries
- Extreme concern for orderliness or placements of objects
- Extreme concern for cleanliness

Compulsion may manifest as:

- Tremendous fears if not acting upon the pressing thoughts, e.g., not supposed to touch the doorknob with bare hands or not to sit without putting something on the seat
- Needing to check and re-check
- Unreasonable counting of things
- Interior pressure to perform the same task over and over again
- Specific, lengthy rituals in doing things
- Demanding of how things have to be done to perfection
- Extreme preoccupation in balancing and keeping things in symmetry
- Dry, cracked hands due to frequent and lengthy hand washing
- Peculiar way of walking due to the need to change or correct steps in response to inner pressure
- Repeatedly putting things in a straight line, aligning, balancing, or putting things in a certain order

Schizophrenia is a chronic, debilitating biochemical disorder characterized by distortion of perception of reality called delusions to disturbing hallucinations. The signs and symptoms may include the following:

- Disorganized and irrational behavior
- Fixated to a particular thought that is not in touch with reality
- Presence of hallucinations (visual, auditory, tactile, olfactory)
- Presence of delusions
- Incoherence and loose association
- Inability to take care of one's personal grooming or hygiene
- Speech is irrational and disorganized in content
- Eyes looking far as if not connected with the surrounding, or suspicious, or refusing to have eye contact
- Peculiar speech, such as talking loudly and carrying a conversation with oneself
- Feeling of depersonalization

Dissociative Identity Disorder (Multiple Personality) is a mental disorder of fragmentation when two or more identities or personalities take control of the behavior of the patient. The patient switches from one identity to the other with distinct traits and given names. The alternate personality seems to be uniquely different from the primary identity. The signs and symptoms may include the following:

- Personality switches with distinct name and identity
- Inability to recall the circumstances surrounding the other person
- There is usually a primary identity with a different personality and name
- Failure to integrate various aspects of identity, memory, personality, and consciousness
- The alternate identity has own history, self-image, personality and name
- There is some type of major trauma and/or abuse involved in the history of the individual
- Situations trigger the switching of personalities, especially major stress
- There are extensive memory gaps in the history of the patient

Depersonalization Personality Disorder is a mental health disorder which the person has a sense of not being real, that parts of the body are not real, the feeling that one is observing self from outside the body, or feeling like one is losing grip on reality or living in a dream. The feelings of depersonalization may include:

- Continuous or recurring feelings that one is an outside observer of one's thoughts, body or parts of the body
- Numbing of one's senses or responses to the world
- Feeling like a robot or feeling like one is living in a dream or in a movie
- The sensation that one is not in control of one's actions, including speaking
- Awareness that one's sense of detachment is only a feeling, and not a reality
- The sense that one's body or parts of the body, like the legs or arms, appear distorted, enlarged or shrunken
- Feeling like one is observing self from above, as if one is floating in the air
- Feeling emotionally disconnected from people about whom one cares

The above signs and symptoms are quick guidelines to the various conditions that may mimic a diabolical condition. For a more detailed description of specifiers for each of the psychiatric conditions, refer to DSM IV-TR or better still the upcoming DSM-5.

APPENDIX D

DIABOLICAL ASSESSMENT

©2012 Dr. Segunda Yanez Acosta

Instruction: **Circle the number** that best describes the intensity of the patient's signs and symptoms.

DIABOLICAL POSSESSION	N/A	MILD	MODERATE	SEVERE	CRIPPLING
Evil has taken over a person against his will	0	1 2 3	4 5 6	7 8 9	10
Involuntary movement propelled by other forces	0	1 2 3	4 5 6	7 8 9	10
Irrational behavior viewed as bizarre and evil	0	1 2 3	4 5 6	7 8 9	10
Eyes darting then rolled up to the top	0	1 2 3	4 5 6	7 8 9	10
Voice changing with eerie, deep, guttural sounds	0	1 2 3	4 5 6	7 8 9	10
Able to predict or know hidden events	0	1 2 3	4 5 6	7 8 9	10
Vile, profane, blasphemous language	0	1 2 3	4 5 6	7 8 9	10
Destruction of holy objects or sacred images	0	1 2 3	4 5 6	7 8 9	10
Disrespect towards or withdrawal from religious	0	1 2 3	4 5 6	7 8 9	10
Extreme, extraordinary strength	0	1 2 3	4 5 6	7 8 9	10
Speaking in and understanding strange tongues	0	1 2 3	4 5 6	7 8 9	10
Bizarre, uncharacteristic ritual against person's will	0	1 2 3	4 5 6	7 8 9	10
Supernatural power to move against nature	0	1 2 3	4 5 6	7 8 9	10
Body arches rigidly and hands are like claws	0	1 2 3	4 5 6	7 8 9	10
Aversion towards or spitting at Holy Eucharist	0	1 2 3	4 5 6	7 8 9	10
Reacting violently to Holy Name of Jesus	0	1 2 3	4 5 6	7 8 9	10
DIABOLICAL OBSESSION					
Tormented by unrelenting evil thoughts	0	1 2 3	4 5 6	7 8 9	10
Extreme preoccupation with demonic ideas	0	1 2 3	4 5 6	7 8 9	10
Extreme, bizarre display of religiosity	0	1 2 3	4 5 6	7 8 9	10
Tormented by hearing eerie, unexplainable noises	0	1 2 3	4 5 6	7 8 9	10
Direct attack by evil on internal organs	0	1 2 3	4 5 6	7 8 9	10
Diabolical visions, images eliciting fear in the person	0	1 2 3	4 5 6	7 8 9	10
Unexplained physical illness	0	1 2 3	4 5 6	7 8 9	10
Evil sexual stimulation and feeling of penetration	0	1 2 3	4 5 6	7 8 9	10
Other senses are attacked by evil (e.g., taste, smell)	0	1 2 3	4 5 6	7 8 9	10
DIABOLICAL OPPRESSION					
Frequent, unexplained obstacles in life	0	1 2 3	4 5 6	7 8 9	10
Feeling physically blocked by some forces	0	1 2 3	4 5 6	7 8 9	10
Attacked in finances, relationships, school, job	0	1 2 3	4 5 6	7 8 9	10
Heavy feeling of evil presence pressing on person	0	1 2 3	4 5 6	7 8 9	10
External physically attacked by unseen enemies	0	1 2 3	4 5 6	7 8 9	10
Prevented by unseen enemies from doing things	0	1 2 3	4 5 6	7 8 9	10
Losing spiritually related items or documents	0	1 2 3	4 5 6	7 8 9	10
Harassment by attack on immediate environment	0	1 2 3	4 5 6	7 8 9	10
DIABOLICAL INFESTATION					
Things fly, shake, rattle unexplainably	0	1 2 3	4 5 6	7 8 9	10
Spooky, eerie movements in a room or house	0	1 2 3	4 5 6	7 8 9	10
Peculiar evil smell, sound, or presence on ground	0	1 2 3	4 5 6	7 8 9	10
Objects inhabited by evil forces	0	1 2 3	4 5 6	7 8 9	10
Equipments may act peculiarly scary	0	1 2 3	4 5 6	7 8 9	10
Electricals in house unusually turn on and off	0	1 2 3	4 5 6	7 8 9	10
Weird, scary behavior of animals	0	1 2 3	4 5 6	7 8 9	10

APPENDIX E

SPIRITUAL HEALING FOR SELF AND FAMILY PRAYER TO TAKE AUTHORITY

©2012 Dr. Segunda Yanez Acosta

Heavenly Father, in the name of Jesus Christ, Your Son and our Savior, and by the merits of Christ's suffering, death, and resurrection from the Cross, I take authority and bind all powers and forces of evil in the air, earth, water, underground, fire, electricity, and in all living and inanimate creations. You are the Lord of the entire universe and I acknowledge Your supreme dominion over us. You are our Creator and Savior. I praise You, thank You and wish to glorify You in everything I do. In the name and authority of Jesus Christ, I bind all demonic forces that have come against me, my family, relatives, friends, benefactors, associates, doctors, nurses, patients, priests, religious, seminarians, bishops, our Pope and I seal all of us in the protection of the Precious Blood of our Lord Jesus Christ that was shed for us in the Cross. In the name, power, and authority of Jesus Christ, I bind and command all powers and forces of evil to depart right now from our homes, offices, properties, lands, hospitals, churches, rectories, seminaries, monasteries, and any place I visit. I ask for the Precious Blood of Jesus Christ to cover all these places to be protected from all evil and all harm. Holy Spirit, please transform me and fill up any void in me so that every cell in my body is working to serve and glorify You, my God. Lord, I believe and trust that You heard my prayers. I entrust to You my protection and the protection of all my loved ones. I believe in Your enduring and loving concern for me and all the people I love.

Mother Mary, I seek your loving protection and intercession. Please cover us with the mantle of your love to discourage the attack of the enemies. St. Joseph, I request for your strong and faithful intercession to defend us and protect us from the enemies just as you preserved the Holy Family under your care. I beg you to plead to your Son for our protection. Amen.

HEALING THE FAMILY TREE

©2012 Dr. Segunda Yanez Acosta

Heavenly Father, in the name, power, and authority of Jesus Christ, I come before You as a daughter/son to a Father knowing that You wish nothing more than to ensure my physical and spiritual safety during this treacherous pilgrimage to Heaven. I praise You Father and give You thanks for the countless blessings You bestowed upon me and my loved ones. I pray that these protection and blessings be conferred to all my relatives in my family tree—twelve generations up, twelve generations down, twelve generation sideways—for the healing of all curses, intergenerational spirits, unrepented sins of my forefathers, failed promises, negative emotions, generational vices, hurtful memories, broken relationships, and all emotional, spiritual, physical, and genetic disorders that have plagued my family tree. I ask for the Precious Blood of Your Son, Jesus Christ, to cover all of us and forgive us of our sins of omissions and commissions. I ask that the light of the Holy Spirit purify us from sins of the past and that these stop in this generation and never to follow our children into their generation. I plead Father for Your mercy and compassion for our family lineage into the next generations. We ask all these in Jesus Christ's name and through the intercession of our Holy Mother Mary and St. Joseph. Amen.

EXHIBIT F

EXORCISM LIABILITY RELEASE, MEDICAL, AND TRANSPORTATION AUTHORIZATION FORM

©2012 Dr. Segunda Yanez Acosta

1. We,_____(print) the undersigned Participant, Spouse and Parents/Legal Guardians of the Participant to be EXORCISED do hereby jointly and severally release, forever discharge and agree to hold harmless the Diocese of _____and_____ including but not limited to the Bishop, the exorcist, to their respective staff, volunteers, priests and advisors from and against any and all liability, claims, demands, lawsuits, and expenses arising from the personal injury, sickness, death, or personal property damage of any nature whatsoever which may be incurred or suffered by the undersigned participant or by the participant's spouse, parents or legal guardians or their families before, during, or after the EXORCISM on the following date(s):_____

2. Furthermore, the undersigned jointly and severally also do hereby assume all risk of personal injury, sickness, death, damage, and expenses arising from the participant's participation in all activities associated with the EXORCISM. Further, we do also hereby jointly and severally give authorization and permission for the participant to be given all necessary transportation to and from the EXORCISM location.

3. The undersigned jointly and severally do further hereby agree to indemnify and hold harmless the Diocese of _____and the_____ including but not limited to the Bishop, exorcist, to their respective staff, volunteers, priests and advisors from and against any and all claims, demands, actions, lawsuits, and liabilities, including attorney's fees and expenses sustained by the indemnities as a result of the negligent, willful, unwilful, intentional or unintentional acts of the participant.

4. The undersigned Spouse, Parents/Legal Guardians hereby grant permission for the participant to participate fully in the EXORCISM. We also specifically give our permission to the EXORCISM staff to take the participant to a doctor or hospital should the need arise in the estimation of the staffers. We further hereby authorize the EXORCISM staffers and agree to any needed medical treatments for the participant, including but not limited to hospitalization and we hereby agree fully and completely to assume responsibility for any such medical bills.

   The undersigned acknowledge their responsibility jointly and severally to provide truthful and current health information. The undersigned further understand and acknowledge that their failure to disclose relevant information may cause harm to them and/or their child. The undersigned further jointly and severally represent and warrant that they have provided all materials and important information pertaining to medical, physical, mental, and spiritual condition related to the participant and agree to notify _____ of any changes in the medical, physical, mental or spiritual condition prior to the scheduled EXORCISM event.

   Allergies: _____
   Medical/Mental Conditions: _____
   Physical Limitations: _____
   Medications: _____

5. We further jointly and severally acknowledge that EXORCISM is strictly voluntary, and there is no guarantee of the outcome. Participant agrees and acknowledges by his/her signature below that he/she is to obey all rules and all safety regulations as much as the person has control and that the staff will enforce whatever is necessary to ensure safety of the person even if this may require restraining the individual. Further, the parents/legal guardians also acknowledge and agree that should it be necessary for the participant to return home and come back or the necessity of staying over for a number of days, the participant, spouse, parents/legal guardian who sign below shall assume all responsibilities for the board, lodging, and transportation costs that may be incurred.

Name of Participant to be EXORCISED:_____Parish:_____

Address:_____

Age:_____ Email:_____ Home#_____ cell#_____

SIGNATURE AND AGREEMENT OF PARTICIPANT: _____ Date of Signature: _____

SIGNATURE AND AGREEMENT OF FATHER: _____ Date of Signature: _____

EMERGENCY PHONE NO:_____

SIGNATURE AND AGREEMENT OF MOTHER: _____ Date of Signature: _____

EMERGENCY PHONE NO:_____

SIGNATURE AND AGREEMENT OF SPOUSE: _____ Date of Signature: _____

EMERGENCY PHONE NO:_____

SIGNATURE AND AGREEMENT OF LEGAL GUARDIAN*_____ Date of Signature: _____

EMERGENCY PHONE NO:_____ (As Applicable)

(If both parents' signatures are not available, please provide documentation of legal guardianship or sole custody)

REFERENCES

Abel, Robert: (2006) *Spiritual Warfare Prayers*. Denver, Colorado: Valentine Press.

Abel, Robert: (2006) *The Catholic Warrior*. Denver, Colorado: Valentine Press.

Allen, Thomas B.: (1993) *Possessed*. New York: Bantam Books.

Allen, Thomas B.: (2000) *Possessed: The True Story of an Exorcism*. New York: Universe Press.

American Psychiatric Association: (2000) *Diagnostic and Statistical Manual of Mental Disorders*. Washington, D.C.: American Psychiatric Association.

Amorth, Gabriele: (1999) *An Exorcist Tells His Story*. San Francisco, California: Ignatius Press.

Amorth, Gabriele. (2002) *An Exorcist: More Stories*. San Francisco, California: Ignatius Press.

Aquinas, Thomas: (1952) *Summa Theologica*. Chicago, Illinois: Encyclopedia Britannica.

Aristotle: (1952) *The Works of Aristotle*. Chicago, Illinois: Encyclopedia Britannica, p. 104.

Aumann, Jordan. (1987) *Spiritual Theology*. Manila, Philippines: University of Santo Tomas, pp. 1-5.

Ball, Ann: (1996) *Blessed Miguel Pro 20th century Mexican Martyr*. Illinois: Tan Books.

Byrd, Randolph C: (1988) *Positive therapeutic effects of intercessory prayer in coronary care unit population*. Southern Medical Journal.

Catechism of the Catholic Church. (1994) The dignity of the human person. Liguori, Missouri: Liguori Press, p. 443.

Chesterton, G.K.: (1987) *The Collected Works of G.K. Chesterton*. San Francisco, California: Ignatius Press, pp. 316-317.

Cohen, Bruce J.: (2003) *Theory and Practice of Psychiatry.* Oxford, England: University Press.

Groeschel, Benedict: (1993) *A Still Small Voice: A Practical Guide on Reported Revelations.* San Francisco, California: Ignatius Press.

Groeschel, Benedict: (2006) *The virtue driven life.* Huntington, Indiana: Our Sunday Visitor.

Hardon, John A.: (1996) *What are possession and obsession by the devil?* Lombard, Illinois: Real Presence Association.

Hayes, E.J., Hayes, P.J. and Drummey, J.J.: (2002) *Catholicism and Reason.* Norwood, Massachusetts: C.R. Publications Inc., p. 20.

Kreeft, Peter: (1990) *Summa of the Summa.* San Francisco, California: Ignatius Press, p. 217.

Levin, Jeff: (2001) *God, Faith, and Health.* New York, New York: John Wiley & Sons.

Levin, Jeff and Koenig, Harold: (2005) *Faith, Medicine, and Science.* New York: The Haworth Press Inc.

Lewis, C.S: (1942) *Screwtape Letters.* Ohio: Barbour and Company, pp. 126-130.

Lord, Bob and Penny: (2009) This is My Body, This is My Blood: Miracle of the Eucharist. Arizona: Journeys of Faith.

Matthews, Dale: (1999) *Faith Factor: Is Religion Good for Your Health?* New York, New York: Penguin Publishing.

Martin, Malachi: (1992) *Hostage to the Devil.* San Francisco: Harper Collins Publishers.

Newberg, Andrew B. and D'Aquili, Eugene G.: (1998) The Neuropsychology of Spiritual Experience in *Handbook of Religion and Mental Health.* (ed.) Koenig, H.G. San Diego, California: Academic Press, p. 91.

Nicola, John J.: (1974) *Diabolical Possession and Exorcism.* Rockford, Illinois: Tan Books, p. 47.

Peck, Scott M: (1983) *People of the Lie.* New York, New York: Touchstone.

Peck, Scott M: (1978) *The Road Less Traveled.* New York, New York: Touchstone, pp. 182-186.

Post, Stephen G.: (1998) Ethics, Religion, and Mental Health. In *Handbook of Religion and Mental Health.* (ed.) Koenig, H.G., San Diego, California: Academic Press, p. 21.

Saunders, William: (2003) *Gifts of the Holy Spirit.* Arlington Catholic Herald.

Targ, Elizabeth et al: (1998) *A randomized double-blind study of the effect of distant healing in a population with advanced AIDS. Report of a small scale study*. The Western Journal of Medicine.

The New American Bible. (1991) Woodland Hills, California: Benzinger Publishing Co.

Zimmerman, Mark: (1994) *Diagnosing DSM IV psychiatric disorders in primary care settings*. Greenwich, Rhode Island: Psych Products Press.

NOTICE

The patients used in this book are based on actual cases seen by Dr. Acosta. In order to protect the anonymity of these patients, certain identifying facts were changed to ensure confidentiality of information. Any similarity of these cases with other cases is unintentional and purely coincidental.

Front cover image:

"St. Jerome" by Albrecht Durer (1521)
National Museum of Ancient Art, Lisbon Source: Wikimedia Commons

Chapter drawings by:

Dr. Segunda Yanez Acosta

If the readers wish to provide feedback, share personal stories, or share their professional cases, please mail your letters to:

Seggy Yanez Acosta, Ph.D., P.M.H.C.S., B.C.
S.T.R.E.S.S. CENTRE INC.
10529 Crestwood Drive, Suite 101, Manassas, Virginia 20109

Proceeds of this book will help build Holy Trinity Jubilee Park Inc., a Catholic Park in Northern Virginia as a center for evangelization.

Saint Benedict writing the rules, painting (1926) by Hermann Nigg
(1849-1928) Source: Wikemedia Commons

ST. BENEDICT, PRAY FOR US.

Permission is granted to copy, distribute and/or modify this document under the terms of the *GNU Free Documentation License,* Version 1.2 or any later version published by the *Free Software Foundatio*n; with no Invariant Sections, no Front-Cover Texts, and no Back-Cover Texts. A copy of the license is included in the section entitled *GNU Free Documentation License*. Source: Wikemedia Commons

CPSIA information can be obtained at www.ICGtesting.com
Printed in the USA
BVOW05s0423080514

352844BV00001B/5/P